Mastering SNOWBOARDING

HANNAH TETER
TAWNYA SCHULTZ

Human Kinetics

Library of Congress Cataloging-in-Publication Data

Teter, Hannah.
  Mastering snowboarding / Hannah Teter, Tawnya Schultz.
    p. cm.
  1. Snowboarding. I. Schultz, Tawnya, 1981- II. Title.
  GV857.S57T42 2012
  796.939--dc23

                                2012031908
  ISBN-10: 1-4504-1064-2 (print)
  ISBN-13: 978-1-4504-1064-9 (print)

This publication is written and published to provide accurate and authoritative information relevant to the subject matter presented. It is published and sold with the understanding that the author and publisher are not engaged in rendering legal, medical, or other professional services by reason of their authorship or publication of this work. If medical or other expert assistance is required, the services of a competent professional person should be sought.

The web addresses cited in this text were current as of October 2012, unless otherwise noted.

Acquisitions Editor: Justin Klug; **Developmental Editor:** Carla Zych; **Assistant Editor:** Claire Marty; **Copyeditor:** Patricia Macdonald; **Indexer:** Nan N. Badgett; **Permissions Manager:** Martha Gullo; **Graphic Designer:** Fred Starbird; **Cover Designer:** Keith Blomberg; **Photograph (cover):** JEAN-PIERRE CLATOT/AFP/Getty Images; **Photographs (interior):** pages 9, 13, 19, 22, 26, 27, 28, 29, and 78 courtesy of Burton Snowboards; pages i and 99 courtesy of Matt Corigliano; page 7 courtesy of Trevor Graves; pages 95, 97, 133, 145, 149, 151, and 157 © Erik Hoffman; page 39 Nathan Kendall/Squaw Valley; pages 3, 173, and 182 © Gabe L'Heureux; page ix courtesy of Adam Moran/Burton Snowboards; all other photos © Ben Birk, www.BenBirk.com; **Visual Production Assistant:** Joyce Brumfield; **Photo Production Manager:** Jason Allen; **Art Manager:** Kelly Hendren; **Associate Art Manager:** Alan L. Wilborn; **Illustrations:** © Human Kinetics; **Printer:** Versa Press

We thank Woodward Tahoe/Boreal Mountain Resort in Tahoe, California, and High Cascade Snowboard Camp in Government Camp, Oregon, for assistance in providing the locations for the photo shoots for this book.

Human Kinetics books are available at special discounts for bulk purchase. Special editions or book excerpts can also be created to specification. For details, contact the Special Sales Manager at Human Kinetics.

Printed in the United States of America   10   9   8   7   6   5   4   3   2   1

The paper in this book is certified under a sustainable forestry program.

Human Kinetics
Website: www.HumanKinetics.com

United States: Human Kinetics
P.O. Box 5076
Champaign, IL 61825-5076
800-747-4457
e-mail: humank@hkusa.com

Canada: Human Kinetics
475 Devonshire Road Unit 100
Windsor, ON N8Y 2L5
800-465-7301 (in Canada only)
e-mail: info@hkcanada.com

Europe: Human Kinetics
107 Bradford Road
Stanningley
Leeds LS28 6AT, United Kingdom
+44 (0) 113 255 5665
e-mail: hk@hkeurope.com

Australia: Human Kinetics
57A Price Avenue
Lower Mitcham, South Australia 5062
08 8372 0999
e-mail: info@hkaustralia.com

New Zealand: Human Kinetics
P.O. Box 80
Torrens Park, South Australia 5062
0800 222 062
e-mail: info@hknewzealand.com

E5454

This book is dedicated to Sarah Burke and to all the passionate riders who have made the sport what it is today.

CONTENTS

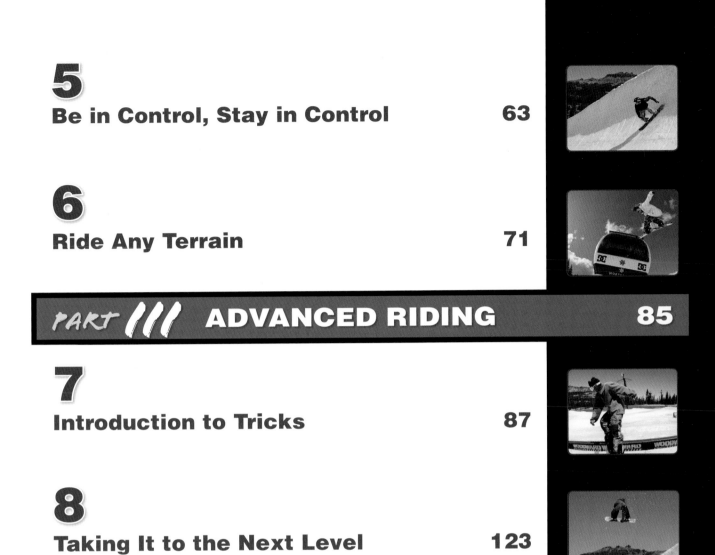

TRICK FINDER

PREFACE

Learning to snowboard can be a life-changing endeavor. Although it can be a bumpy ride at the start with ups and plenty of downs, once people "get it" and develop the ability to link turns on snow, it is easy to get hooked. For some the goal may be to go snowboarding with their friends on weekends; for others it may be to win an Olympic gold medal and have their face on a Wheaties box. Some riders prefer to ride solo, appreciating the beauty all around them; for others the whole point is to share the experience with those they care about. Whatever your motivation to learn how to ride or how to ride better, the opportunity to express yourself as an individual is undoubtedly part of it. The opportunity to challenge yourself and to do what makes *you* happy has made snowboarding what it is today.

Whether you ride frequently or only a few times a year, the process of reaching the level of snowboarding skill you seek can be a long one, involving lots of spills and numbingly cold weather. But as you gain experience, there are plenty of moments along the way that make it all worth it. This is what keeps you going. It's you sliding down the hill with your family during winter vacation. It's locking in a boardslide on a rail for the first time and feeling a sense of accomplishment.

If you want to become an elite snowboarder, there is no secret, no particular path, no right or wrong approach. Success at the professional level is a result of experience, talent, skill, luck, and the drive to improve. The competition and achievement keep you going. It's you against yourself. It's about understanding the backcountry and dropping your first heli line in Alaska and riding the best powder of your life. It's getting your photo published in a snowboard magazine.

Whatever your personal snowboarding goals may be, there will be times when you get discouraged, feel as if it's just too hard, and maybe even scream out loud that you "never want to snowboard again!"

If you don't give up, then you're sure to reap the ultimate reward, whatever that may be for you. Maybe it will be recognizing that being strapped on a piece of wood in the dead of winter makes you feel more alive than ever before. Maybe it will be standing on top of a mountain, appreciating the stillness and beauty, then speeding down the slope as fast as humanly possible, feeling the rush of cold air against your skin, being engulfed by a giant wave of snow you've just created, riding away, and wanting nothing more than to do it all over again.

Snowboarding is freedom in its rawest form.

ACKNOWLEDGMENTS

I would like to thank all the great coaches and instructors I have had in snowboarding, especially my brothers, who got me into the sport when I was a little girl and were among my most influential coaches these last 15 years, and the US team coaches: Ricky Bower, Bud Keene, Mike Jankowski, and Tommy Czeschin.

I'd also like to thank my amazing sponsors, who have helped get me where I am today—Jake and Donna Carpenter, Susie Floros, Bryan Knox, Kevin Keller, Adam Moran, Gabe L'Heureux, Anne Marie and Greg Dacyshyn, and Karen Yankowski at Burton; Randy Torcom at Anon; Todd Ballard and Adam Instone at GoPro; Mindi Befu and John Rice at Sierra at Tahoe Resort; and Erin Magee and Daniel Goldstein at Pantech.

Thanks to my agent and brother Amen and to my amazing Octagon support team: Peter Carlisle, Michael Fudzinski, Ben Morrill, Drew Johnson, Cheryl Herbert, Kelly Cyr, Kurt Grazer, Caitlin Huggins, and Scott Gaffield.

Special thanks to my mom and dad for encouraging me to live my dream.

Extra special thanks to everyone who picks up this book and finds another reason to get outside and shred the gnar!

Hannah

First and foremost I would like to thank Mia Troy-Vowell for giving me the opportunity to do this project. I will be forever grateful. Having my first book be about snowboarding, one of my biggest passions in life, is very humbling and fulfilling.

Thanks to everyone at Human Kinetics, especially Justin and Carla, for making this project a reality. Snowboarding is something that needs to be shared with the world, and this is such a great starting point. Thank you for the endless hours you put in and your support in guiding a new author like me to fulfill one of her childhood dreams. Now we just gotta get you out of the office and into the mountains!

Endless thanks to my mom, dad, grandparents, sister and entire family for their constant interest, love, and support throughout this year-long endeavor. I couldn't have done it without you. Grandma Ginny, I know you would have been so proud to have seen the finished project.

Thank you to my best friend Kara, who is the best support system and roommate ever, and to Brian Bell, I.J., Brendon, the O.G. 118 crew, Steve K., Heather, Hillary and so many more for all you do.

Thanks to all the riders involved in the book—you killed it—and to Hannah and Amen for making it happen.

Thanks also to everyone at Burton who helped gather photos and information under tight deadlines; the crews at Woodward, HCSC, and Windell's; all the photographers who contributed, especially Ben Birk; and to all the riders who have ever inspired me.

There's no way to thank you all, but what you have done has helped shape my life. I hope I can pass that on.

Tawnya

INTRODUCTION

Whether you're interested in trying snowboarding for the first time or have been doing it for years, by picking up this book you've made it clear that you want to know more. Maybe you already live in the mountains, or maybe you live far from them, somewhere in a sweltering desert, and can only dream of snow.

No matter where you are in the world or what your snowboarding background, this guide is built to help you understand everything there is to know about the sport. First off, it covers the history of the sport and how snowboarding came about. Did you know it took years for snowboarding to be allowed at most resorts? You'll find out why and hear about the colorful, innovative people who were integral in making snowboarding what it is today.

Next, we'll dive into what equipment and gear you need and what to buy to look like a real snowboarder. The ever-expanding array of products on the market can be confusing, and we're here to help. We'll break down the technical jargon and tell you what you need to know about hard goods and soft goods, giving you the knowledge and confidence to find the right equipment to suit your style and needs.

If you've never strapped a foot on a snowboard, there's a chapter dedicated to giving you a leg up. Find out what to expect on your first day, and learn insider tips on carving and linking turns. You'll be a snowboarder in no time. All it takes is a little practice and confidence.

There is information on how to improve your control and master the basics. Once you've learned the guidelines on rider etiquette and dialed in your turns, it's time for our tips on taking your skills to the park and backcountry.

Park riding has exploded over the last decade, and resorts have taken notice, building features of all shapes and sizes for riders of all abilities, from beginner to pro. If you've always wanted to hit a rail or have previously been scared to step it up to that bigger jump, the photos and step-by-step instructions in the chapters on hitting tricks will help you make your vision a reality.

There's also a lot to learn when it comes to riding out of bounds, and we'll let you know what to expect and how to be prepared for the unexpected. You'll be ready to shred untouched powder safely and smartly before you know it.

Curious about all the tricks you see advanced and professional snowboarders pull off? The tricks guide explains in step-by-step fashion many of the moves featured in competitions.

With insight from the pros who know the competitive side of the sport best, the final chapter highlights the dedication required to become a professional and gives you an idea of just what it takes to make it in the industry.

From the crazy idea that it might be possible to surf on snow to one of the most popular sports in the winter Olympics, snowboarding has come a long way, emerging as one of the fastest-growing action sports over the past few decades. Whether you want to give this growing winter pastime a try, take on a more challenging run at your favorite resort, or stand atop a podium someday, we hope this guide gets you itching to hit the slopes. Good luck and happy shredding . . . and *don't* break a leg!

PART 1

Before You Begin

Before strapping in and hitting the slopes, take some time to learn about the sport and what you are in for. Part I leads off with some information on the history of snowboarding and how it has developed into a worldwide sensation. We'll introduce you to the people who made it possible and fill you in on how the equipment has evolved over the years.

Then in chapter 2 we'll help you check out the variety of snowboarding hard goods and soft goods and figure out how to choose what's right for you. We'll also explain how to assemble and set up your board and what you need to do to maintain it.

It helps to know ahead of time what it's like on the slopes and how to succeed to the fullest. Chapter 3 offers plenty of pointers and inside tips on learning the concepts and making the most of your time. You are on your way to becoming a snowboarder!

History of Snowboarding

The foundation on which snowboarding was built is a fairy tale of sorts, complete with an evil emperor, lots of characters, and a happy ending of course. When referencing the evolution of a time, place, or thing, the true timeline of it all is often hazy—colored by personal impressions and hindsight. Although the same goes for snowboarding, with plenty of he said, she said, the sport is young in comparison to most, so the history is relatively fresh and clear. Many of the sport's founders are still living, breathing, and shredding with the younger generations today.

Modern-day snowboarding is quite different from the original idea thought up sometime in the mid-1960s. In the beginning, no one was thinking about carving big mountains, boosting 50-foot (15 m) tabletops, or nose-sliding rails. The inception was a man dreaming up a toy to please his daughter. On Christmas Day in 1965, in Muskegon, Michigan, a man named Sherman Poppen decided to drill together two 36-inch (91 cm) skis he had bought at a local drugstore. All his daughter Wendy wanted was to be able to stand up on her sled, and Poppen was determined to grant her wish. The basic sled with a rope that he created was an instant hit in the neighborhood. Kids were soon asking Poppen to build them one too, and his inventor mentality began taking over. Poppen's wife named the toy a "Snurfer" since the act of riding down the hill resembled surfing on the snow. Within a year Poppen sold the Snurfer idea to Brunswick (yes, the bowling ball manufacturer), and more than one million units were sold over the next 10 years for $10 to $30 each.

Snurfing (which is similar to what is now known as noboarding) took shape, and contests drew crowds of hundreds at local resorts. There were in fact pro "Snurfers" and a media following, but it didn't catch on in a big way. Poor marketing didn't help, and the Snurfing fad came and went with hardly a trace. It did leave an impression on some key people, though.

Snurfing Gives Way to Snowboarding

Meanwhile, in 1970 an east coast surfer was conjuring up a little something of his own. Inspired by messing around in the schoolyard, sliding sideways with lunch trays strapped to his feet—probably out of boredom—Dimitrije Milovich took his newfound form of fun to the garage and created what he called a snowboard. Milovich soon linked up with Jersey surfboard shaper Wayne Stoveken, who was already working on snow–surfboard prototypes. Within a few short years, Milovich had patented and designed the Swallowtail, and in 1976 he founded Winterstick, the first snowboard company.

Snowboards were originally made for powder. Unable to hold an edge on hardpack, snowboards were meant for cruising and riding the white waves of the snowy mountains. There were fins on the bottom, and they were shaped much like a surfboard at that time. The stance was set back, with both feet angled to the front. The rider wore hard ski or mountaineering boots, and the outfits were a whole different story. In some ways, this phase is considered the glory days of snowboarding. The sport was in its infancy, hardly a blip on anyone's radar. No one had any expectations of the sport's becoming a worldwide phenomenon; the pioneers of snowboarding were just out to do something cool and different and have a good time. These early times helped establish the spirit of the sport.

Two men from opposite coasts who caught the Snurfing sensation decades ago are still dominant in the world of snowboarding today: Jake Burton Carpenter and Tom Sims.

At age 23, Carpenter was on the fast track for Wall Street success, after finishing school in economics, when he took a detour. With snowboarding still looking like a fad, Carpenter had a dream that his passion for riding on snow could become a legitimate sport. "The minute I got on a Snurfer and rode it, I knew there was a sport there," said Carpenter in a CNBC interview. With the vision of building his own boards and making snowboarding something more than a fad, he decided to ditch the tie, head back to the mountains of Vermont, and try to figure out how to manufacture a prototype he had built with wooden planks and water ski bindings. Carpenter decided to establish his own company, Burton Boards, in 1977, where he began to hand-build boards in his barn. Carpenter would drive to resorts and try to sell the boards out of the trunk of his car to kids in the parking lot. Over the next few years, Carpenter kept his head up, continued to set goals, and convinced ski shop owners to sell Burton snowboards. It was a slow climb, but his hard work and determination most certainly paid off. After 35 years, Carpenter is still a major advocate and innovator of the sport and is active in running the world's leading snowboard brand.

In 1979 there was a Snurfing contest being held in Rockford, Michigan. Jake Burton Carpenter decided to make his way there and enter on his own board. Little did he know the Snurfing community would refuse to allow it. After some negotiating, event directors added an "open" category, where Carpenter was the only competitor, obviously taking top honors in the event. Carpenter was slowly but aggressively paving the way for the sport. He lobbied for years for snowboarding to be allowed at resorts and one by one they started to come around.

Even though boards were difficult and expensive to make, Carpenter truly believed snowboarding was going to become a sensation. On the east coast, however, the sport was still very Alpine-esque, with hard boots and racing at the top of the agenda. Snowboarding on the west coast was a whole other story.

The Freestyle Movement

In the late 1970s over in California, former skateboard champ Tom Sims was busy testing out his "ski board" on local slopes. Sims, who was also an avid surfer, was motivated by the possibility of riding a board year-round. With his resources as a skateboard maker and a brand already intact, Sims decided to make moves with his own snowboard prototype in Tahoe. With Chuck Barfoot, who had figured out how to use fiberglass in snowboard production, by his side, Sims was a legitimate seller. He just had to find people to buy. Mike Chantry, then skateboard park manager in Reno, was familiar with the Sims brand and began bringing pro skateboarders up to Tahoe to ride Sims snowboards. Needless to say, Sims brought the surf and skate influence to snowboarding, and locals such as Terry Kidwell, Bob Klein, and Mark Anolik were intrigued.

The old Tahoe City dump in North Lake Tahoe has the distinction of being the location of the first snowboard quarterpipe and the birthplace of freestyle snowboarding. When the trash had been bulldozed out, what was left was a U shape in the backwoods that accumulated an abundance of snow in the winter. The spot became the local shred and hang spot for riders looking to get their fix. Kidwell, Klein, and others would hit the dump after school and push the snow by hand and with shovels to perfect the drop-in so they could ride up and down the wall, just as they would on a skateboard. Word spread. Skateboard photographers began venturing to Tahoe to snap photos of the big-name skateboarders who were trying this newfound sport. Soon-to-be snowboarding superstars gained notoriety in skateboarding and surfing magazines, and interest began building.

Tom Sims began growing a team of kids who were basically unpaid advocates, since at the time there was no real money in snowboarding. He would send them free product, and they would send Sims feedback on improving the decks. There were still fins on the bottom, and the "bindings" were made with cross-country ski plates, no highbacks and straps to hold the feet down. Since holding an edge became a concern, Sims and his crew began cutting metal edging off of skis and gluing it down the side of the decks. Problem solved. Well, progress was moving in the right direction at least.

The Red-Headed Stepchild Makes Good

Carpenter was one of the first to truly push resorts to allow snowboarders to ride chairlifts. The ski industry was more than a little wary given the commonly held image of skateboarding and youth culture at the time. With resorts and ski executives slamming doors and basically laughing at the idea of allowing these "boarders" to mess up their slopes and precious powder, snowboarders continued to feel like and to be viewed as outsiders.

In 1981, at Ski Cooper in Leadville, Colorado, the first ever snowboard contest was held. King of the Mountain, founded by shop owner Richard Christiansen, was a hit, yet Ski Cooper didn't allow riders to take the lifts. They were sure the sport was a fad. Guess they were wrong.

The following year, the first National Snowsurfing Championships (NSC) were held at Suicide Six ski area in Woodstock, Vermont. Downhill racers were clocked at 30 miles per hour (48 km/h), half the speed of what is possible today but a milestone at the time. The television and magazine attention the resort received because of the event convinced the management to allow the side-slippers for good. Progress! Three years later, in 1985, the NSC became the U.S. Open of Snowboarding, owned and operated by Burton, and was moved to Stratton, Vermont. Back then the contest featured only downhill racing, and speed suits were all the rage, but it was the beginning of what would become one of the most exciting events of the season. It is now the place where the top riders in superpipe and slopestyle are crowned, while wearing loose-fitting, casual attire in keeping with the current snowboarding mindset and lifestyle.

In 1983 Tom Sims held the first World Snowboarding Championships at Soda Springs in Tahoe. He decided to add halfpipe in addition to downhill and slalom. He's noted as the first person to introduce the freestyle aspect to competition.

As media attention began to build in magazines and movies, and as other manufacturers started seeking their own ways to profit, the ski industry began to come around. In 1985 Breckenridge in Colorado, Soda Springs, Stratton, and Mammoth Mountain in Southern California tried their luck at allowing snowboarders. The following year Stratton was the first resort to offer snowboard instruction and rentals. The sport was getting its wings.

While things in North America were taking shape, Jose Fernandes in Switzerland had taken notice. He had been working on his own prototypes and following the rise of the sport in the United States. Fernandes decided to order a board. Winterstick had spread across the pond, and the snowboard buzz was gaining momentum.

In 1982 France's Les Arcs 2000 invited snowboarders to its new resort, making it the first in Europe. Another step in the right direction. Frenchman Regis Rolland was another early European pioneer. He landed a role as the "good guy" snowboarder versus the villain skiers in the cult classic *Apocalypse Snow*. The film served as a prelude for what would go on for decades: snowboarders riding alone while skiers ridiculed.

Freestyler Terje Haakonsen, shown here competing in the 1992 U.S. Open, helped move the sport forward in the United States and Europe.

In 1985 Hot Snowboards in France released the One Sixty, a board with edges and a parabolic sidecut allowing riders to carve into turns. Many manufacturers followed suit.

In 1987 Europe hosted its own World Championships of Snowboarding, and the rest as they say is history. Fernandes later became president of the ISF (International Snowboard Federation). One of the most notable pros from Europe is freestyle legend Terje Haakonsen. Haakonsen has become a staple of the sport, most notably creating the Ticket to Ride Series (TTR), which helps keep snowboarding in the hands of real snowboarders as opposed to businesspeople and ski affiliates. With Haaksonsen's help, TTR developed a method of quantifying riders' abilities throughout the season, awarding them points at certified events based on their standings, and giving riders an ultimate prize money package at the U.S. Open championships. A collection of dedicated people from around the globe transformed snowboarding into a noteworthy endeavor. (People even write books about it now!)

Clipping the Fins and Breaking Out

In the mid- to late eighties, board manufacturers began changing the game. The whole fin idea no longer made sense. Refinements and advancements were made to the shape, and metal edges became the norm. In 1985 snowboard construction shifted, becoming more modern and paving the way for the boards we know today. The freestyle scene was growing, and Burton saw potential. Instead of setting the bindings on the back of the board, stances were drilled more centered. Although riders still rode with their feet close together and pointed toward the front of the board, the freestyle movement truly began to develop and thrive.

As the boards evolved, other changes followed. Shops in 1986 released the first set of soft boots produced by Burton. Ski and mountaineering boots weren't going to cut it anymore. Riders needed to be able to flex and bend in order to catch air and attempt tricks, and hard boots were much too stiff to do any of that. There was not much room to grow, and it was time for manufacturers to think outside of Alpine racing and to create equipment based on the kinds of moves snowboarders wanted to do, such as jumps, spins, slashes, and grabs. In 1987 Burton introduced the first twin-tip freestyle board. This freestyle-specific deck remains a staple today, with its identical tip and tail, enabling the rider to feel the same riding in both directions, and making learning and landing tricks easier. The innovation in freestyle equipment of softer boards, boots, and bindings was a radical departure that signaled the pace and scope of the changes to come. The revolution had begun.

Resorts slowly but surely began coming around, and snowboarders no longer had to hike hills and build their own halfpipes. Resorts began hand-carving ditch-like walls and jumps. Although skiers still ruled the slopes, snowboarding was being recognized as a legitimate sport on its own. Production of boards and gear took off in Europe, and sales increased as more kids caught wind of the new action sport. Snowboarding was finding its own identity, as youthful riders started rocking baggy pants and flannels along with a laid-back attitude and an adventurous, independent spirit. The rebel image—sparked by the fact that snowboarders were viewed as outsiders from the start—took root and was embraced by the snowboarders themselves, and the pros began marketing themselves accordingly. The early snowboarders were typically

As riders became more adventurous, the boards evolved to meet changing demands.

boys in their teens who were more than happy to set themselves apart from the old people who had held the ski industry and the slopes in their grasp for decades.

Magazines had sprouted up, including *Absolutely Radical* in 1985, but it wasn't until *Transworld Snowboarding* and *Snowboarder Magazine* launched that excitement about the sport truly began to spread. Both publications had a reputable image within the skate and surf markets, and snowboarding began taking over as "the next big thing" in the board-sports world. Now kids who had to drive hours or even days to hit the slopes could read about, and better yet see, soon-to-be superstars for themselves.

While more and more people became familiar with the sport, videographers began to document and produce legit snowboard films. Early reels were basically grainy and shaky footage of friends following each other around the mountain, complete with music and now-considered cheesy graphics. Being able to watch someone snowboard, to visualize and copy the moves, was pure bliss for many. The Internet then was obviously nothing like what it is today. Movies would legitimately take a year to produce, edit, and manufacture, and every fall the movies would hit shop shelves right before the season started. Skateboard filmers and photographers gravitated toward the new challenge of shooting on snow and capturing the essence, while legendary ski filmmaker Warren Miller added a few snowboarders to his roster. Soon, production companies including Mack Dawg and Standard were founded, releasing classic videos such as *New Kids on the Twock*; *The Hard, the Hungry, and the Homeless*; *Double Decade*; and the *Totally Board* series. Snowboard segments in videos documented how professionals were progressing the sport, giving kids a lesson in style and maneuvers. Pro riders were honored if they were given the opportunity to appear in a big-name video made by Mack Dawg or Standard, which set the standard that everyone else followed. Locking down shots in a video was a chance for riders to showcase their talents outside of the competitive world. Eventually there were two types of riders: those who competed and those who filmed. It was (and still is) quite difficult to be successful in both. Riders on film generally ride big mountain, backcountry terrain, and urban features. As snowboarding began to truly emerge across the world, competitive snowboarding got fierce, and it was time to think bigger—and that meant the Olympics.

By the mid-1990s, the USASA (United States of America Snowboard Association) had members across the United States, and parents began driving their kids miles to the mountains for competitions on weekends. Riders qualified for national contests through contests at local resorts and hoped to be successful enough to win an invitation to the nationals held during the spring. This is how many pros got their start, including Danny Kass, Scotty Lago, Hannah Teter, Kelly Clark, the Mitrani brothers, and the most widely recognized snowboarder of all, Shaun White. Riders gained sponsors by doing well at nationals and were then invited to even bigger events, including the U.S. Open of Snowboarding and the Winter X Games.

In 1998, snowboarding made its Olympic debut in Nagano, Japan (table 1.1). Halfpipe and giant slalom were the only disciplines. Since then, snowboard cross has been added. The scale in which snowboarding has become publicized because of the Olympics is vast and hard to measure. The Winter Games in Sochi, Russia, in 2014 are set to debut slopestyle for the first time, lending a grander scale to the sport. Snowboarding's potential still seems endless.

TABLE 1.1 SNOWBOARDING OLYMPIANS

	Men's halfpipe	Women's halfpipe
1998 Olympic winners	Gold—Gian Simmen, Switzerland Silver—Daniel Franck, Norway Bronze—Ross Powers, United States	Gold—Nicola Thost, Germany Silver—Stine Brun Kjeldaas, Norway Bronze—Shannon Dunn, United States
2002 Olympic winners	Gold—Ross Powers, United States Silver—Danny Kass, United States Bronze—Jarrett Thomas, United States	Gold—Kelly Clark, United States Silver—Doriane Vidal, France Bronze—Fabienne Reuteler, Switzerland
2006 Olympic winners	Gold—Shaun White, United States Silver—Danny Kass, United States Bronze—Markku Koski, Finland	Gold—Hannah Teter, United States Silver—Gretchen Bleiler, United States Bronze—Kjersti Buaas, Norway
2010 Olympic winners	Gold—Shaun White, United States Silver—Peetu Piiroinen, Finland Bronze—Scotty Lago, United States	Gold—Torah Bright, Australia Silver—Hannah Teter, United States Bronze—Kelly Clark, United States

CHAPTER 2

Choosing and Assembling the Proper Equipment

Equipment can make or break your snowboarding experience, but the array of products is constantly expanding, the prices are daunting, and the technology changes every year. Is doling out the big bucks for high-end boots worth it? Is it possible to find appealing colors and graphics without sacrificing quality?

Don't panic. To assist you in your quest for the perfect setup, we've broken it all down, item by item. Whether you're adding to your collection of gear or just starting out, there are some principles and guidelines that will make shopping less stressful.

Rule number one: Don't rush into buying everything at once. Do some light reading to learn about the latest technological breakthroughs and what they can truly do for you. By reading reviews and seeing a product in print, it may help you discover what you are looking for. Just know, the most expensive product is not necessarily the best, and a low price isn't always a bargain. Name-brand gear has notoriety and works well for a reason. Products are thoroughly tested to ensure consumers are purchasing a high-quality item. Doing a little research can go a long way.

If you're able to hit up a demo at a local resort, do it. This is the ultimate place to test out different boards, boots, and bindings to see and feel the difference for yourself before making a decision.

Go into a legit snowboard shop, talk with employees who ride, and try stuff on. Don't be afraid to ask questions and find out the differences in all the varieties of products. Talk to real people to see what they think about the products. You might even make some friends while you're at it! Shopping locally is also a great way to support the snowboarding community. Sure, some items may be cheaper on the Web, but the experience of going into a shop and talking with people of similar interests is priceless—and by purchasing from local retailers, you help ensure they'll be there to help you and other snowboarders in the future.

Finally, after gathering information and advice, remember to stop and think about how well it applies to you. Consider your unique size, shape, and weight as well as your personal style, level of skill and experience, and preferred terrain. Also think about how often you ride and how much you can reasonably afford to spend.

Now we'll get into the specific products you'll need: hard goods, protection, and soft goods.

Hard Goods

The main components of snowboarding are the board, boots, and bindings. These three elements are the trifecta, the holy grail, or simply the hard goods that you must put time and effort into choosing before proceeding. If you've never been snowboarding, it doesn't make sense to go right out and purchase an entire setup because you don't know what kind of riding you enjoy or how much you are actually going to use it. But it is important to know what you should look for once you decide to invest in your own gear.

Because boots should be your first priority, we'll go over the proper way to pick boots first and go from there. Finding the perfect pair of boots will make you a better rider and a happier one. Next, we'll explain buying power and what you need to look for when picking out a board that suits your preferred riding style. To help you succeed, we'll talk about finding the right bindings to fit your board and mesh with your deck. Later in the chapter, we'll go over soft goods and how to keep your equipment in good shape for years to come.

Boots

Boots are the most important part of any setup. This can't be stressed enough. They're also the most difficult item of all to find a proper fit, and even when you think they're comfortable in the store, ask a lot of questions. Boots can take days and even weeks to break in. Depending on how many days you snowboard a year, your feet could be hurting for some time if you've opted for a stiff pair.

The best advice is to take the time to find boots that you love first and then find the board and bindings of your dreams. Obtaining the right boots is no easy task, but with the right amount of information you should be on the right track. The number one thing you want to focus on is comfort. You are going to be spending hours at a time in these things, so they need to be not just manageable but dreamy. The price range for boots is somewhere between $100 and $400, though the average is around $250.

There is new snowboard boot tech coming out all the time, and no two boots are the same. Although lace-ups used to be the norm, boots now feature endless mechanisms for tightening and locking. Boots are consciously designed from the outside in. They must be not only durable but functional too. Tread on the bottom is important to prevent slipping when walking through icy parking lots and in piles of snow. The heel of the boot is usually about a half inch to an inch (a couple of centimeters) from where your

The Burton Hail is a basic, lace-up, men's boot made for comfort.

actual heel will sit. The space between is typically filled with compression materials or a gel of some sort to help soften landings and support the heel during heel-side turns.

Fit

The toe of the boot is one of the most intricate parts since this spot tends to suffer the most wear. Your toes are also the first thing that gets cold, so making sure there is enough padding and warming material is important as well. The outsoles of most boots use tested waterproof materials, ensuring no moisture will get to your feet. While the outside material can often appear wet, the inside will stay dry because of the wicking properties of the material used.

When trying on boots, try both the right and left at the same time, and tighten them up completely. Since many boots have fancy mechanisms, it's good to figure out how they work beforehand in the store, and once you purchase them, learn to lace them up again at home, instead of making people wait for you on the hill. There are usually two or three parts you'll have to tighten down: an inside liner that has a string pull lock, and an outside closure system using features such as traditional laces, Boa wire, Velcro, or Speed Zone-type zip cords. Manufacturers offer a variety of lacing options, so testing out different systems while you're in the store and figuring out what you like is worth the effort.

Stand in your snowboard stance and bend your knees. Feel the compression of the boot, and feel how it bends through the foot and the ankle. Bend up and down a few times, like you would strapped in on your board, to get an idea of how the boot will feel in the binding. Is it stiff or super soft? Remember that most boots do take some time to break in, so if you think they feel stiff right away, walk around in them as much as you can to gauge their fit and comfort level. Notice pressure points and any section that may be poking into your foot. If they seem awkward right away, try another pair to tell the difference. The boots shouldn't make you feel pain just by walking in them.

Your big toe should brush the front of the boot when you bend your knees. If it is squished, then you need to up your size. You should have little movement of your foot inside the boot—you want the boots to fit snugly because they will stretch a little. If they hurt right away, then again try a few other pairs and compare. The shop employee should be able to answer any questions you may have about fits of specific boots.

Walk around for a bit. How is the comfort overall? Is your heel lifting at all? Heel lift is the most common problem when searching for the right boot. Your heel should lift minimally, if at all, and should feel held down in place. If your heel lifts up, it will compromise your maneuverability on your board and cause problems when making turns and landing tricks.

Liners and Inserts

Liners or inserts are an inside piece in the boot that is often removable. The outside is considered the shell. Liners can be replaced if they are wearing down. The boot itself usually can't. Liners shouldn't have to be removed unless they get wet or soggy from being worn all day and you want to dry them out. No outer shell of a boot is completely waterproof , which is why there are different parts of a boot to help absorb any moisture that may get through. The system as a whole helps keep your feet dry and warm.

Most liners, if they aren't made to be heat molded, will fit better and more securely to your foot once they have been worn a few times. Keep that in mind, and try on as many pairs as possible to get a good idea of which boots fit your feet best. Right out of the box, a boot should feel pretty comfortable overall.

There are several types of liners, falling into three categories:

○ Stock (nonmoldable): You will find these liners in low-price-point boots. Stock liners are made with less pliable materials and don't provide as much stability on hardpack and landings. The boot will usually still conform to your foot, but it won't provide much support or last as long as a moldable liner.

○ Moldable: Moldable liners are standard in most boots. Although they may be pricier, they offer a shorter break-in period and more of a custom fit. The liner molds to your foot by your own foot's heat and shape.

○ Heat moldable: Heated molds provide a true custom fit instantly. To get the best fit possible, they must be heated with a heating mechanism found in-store or in an oven or similar device at home (follow the directions carefully), although they will work with body heat over time as well.

Heat-moldable liners further assist in getting a secure and comfortable fit. Just like getting a suit tailored, a heat-moldable liner will make the boot fit perfectly to your foot. Heat molds can take care of some of the lift issue if you are experiencing that. If a shop carries heat-moldable boots, you should be able to mold and fit them right in the store. Once you decide you want to purchase the boots, the employee will take out the liners and place them on a heater. Then you put the liners on your feet, which helps the liners mold to the shape of your feet.

Boots with high-end liners offer better support for your foot overall. Although boots with more intricate liners are often more expensive because of the materials and mechanisms used, they will generally last longer. Pricing will vary, and a more expensive higher-end boot may cost as much as $400. However, a less expensive boot may feel better and may work for you just as well.

Depending on your riding style, how much you ride, what types of terrain you prefer, and so on, the retailer should be able to lead you to the right type of boot. Most riders use the liners that come in the boots, but some will add a foot bed, such as Superfeet or Outlast, to get a better adjustment and to help with arch support because most liners are flat on the bottom. Most liners are made of ethylene vinyl acetate (EVA)—a lightweight, moldable polymer similar to foam rubber. Ask the sales attendant about the various liners and what the difference is if you are confused. Sometimes the difference between liners is obvious, and sometimes it isn't. If there is a range in pricing, ask why.

Flex

A midflex boot will often do the trick for most beginner to intermediate riders. Find out the flex rating of the boots you are trying on. Usually a 1 is softest and a 10 is stiffest. Riders who prefer stiffer boots choose higher-rated boots for added support. Stiffer boots also tend to last more days on the hill, although they do have a longer break-in period. Because stiffer boots can help absorb hard landings, they are useful in big mountain conditions and if you are taking bigger risks on jumps.

Breaking in boots can take a day or several, depending on how much you wear them and the boot itself. Feeling pain throughout the feet is common the first few days out in any boot, so don't question your selection just because your feet hurt. If the pain is too much, loosen the boots a little. Having them tightened all the way may be causing some of the pain.

Some riders like to get an added insole for the bottom of their boots that's made exactly for their foot or one that matches the arch of their foot and the support they are looking for. As mentioned before, it may be good to get insoles since this will help with arch support and give your boots extra mileage.

Some riders prefer lace-ups to speed lacing since they think they have more control with the fit. It's again a matter of preference. Most boots provide a combination of self-lacing and a speed system to offer options for different parts of the foot. A rider might like a looser fit in the ankle, yet a tight fit through the foot. Try different methods if you aren't sure. If you hate taking the time to lace, then consider a Speed Zone system or Boa. Try a few different models to see which one suits your needs best.

Get proper snowboard-specific socks that are made to wick away moisture, since your feet will sweat throughout the day. Wearing two or five pairs of regular socks will only make your foot colder and wear out your liner. Wearing your boots all day can sometimes lead to swamp foot, meaning your foot and liner will be somewhat damp by the end of the day. Make sure you take your boots off after riding and dry them at night on a boot dryer or next to (but not close enough to burn) a fireplace. This will ensure your liners dry all the way so if you ride the next day you won't be putting your foot into something that's already wet.

A system you will see in today's higher-end boots is Recco. Taken from the military search and rescue term *reconnaissance*, Recco is an added feature for those who ride off-piste (out of bounds) terrain. If a rider gets buried in an avalanche, the Recco reflector helps rescuers find the person with an electronic device used by most snow patrols. It's a safety feature some riders like to have for added piece of mind. Look for the emblem and logo if you're a backcountry-specific rider. Recco is also available on outerwear.

When you're outside in the cold all day, it is difficult to keep your feet warm. Although most boots do an exceptional job retaining heat and keeping your feet from going numb, some models of boots take the added precaution of including a battery-operated heater. Burton added these to its boots a few years back, and they have solved many riders' circulation issues. Look into the heating system if you live in frigid climates or ride in places where it never gets above freezing.

To get yourself psyched and to break in your boots, wear them around your house for an hour or two and get used to the feel of them. You can even put on your whole kit if you'd like and pretend it's snowing outside. Pop in a snowboard video and practice some maneuvers. Who cares if people judge you? It's time to shred . . . almost.

Boards

Buying a board is like buying a car. You are faced with an overwhelming number of brands and styles, features and add-ons, and sometimes even a pesky salesclerk who wants to get rid of inventory and make that sale. Buying a board straight off the shelf is a bad idea for several reasons. You wouldn't buy a car without test driving it or at least learning enough about it to be comfortable spending your hard-earned dollars, would you? Unless you've used the exact model before, be wary. If you haven't been able to ride the board beforehand but have a good feeling about it, you may just want to go with it. If you've done enough research and talked to riders who recommend the board, then consider it. Just don't be pressured into buying something you're not sure about. If you know how much you're willing to spend, what the typical costs are, and what you really need, you will be able to stay within your price range. If you're a beginner, make sure you check out the beginner boards. They sell them for a reason. Know your skill level, and get a board that is appropriate for that level.

Buying a board is an exciting investment. If you do it right, you could end up with a piece of wood that you might quite possibly consider a best friend. It's more than a piece of wood, though; a snowboard represents freedom and fun. Acquiring the ultimate setup may take years, but keep in mind the point isn't to have the newest and best equipment, it's to get out in the mountains and have some fun.

It used to be boards were pretty much all the same. There was some basic technology, and other manufacturers tried to duplicate it. Over the past decade, snowboard technology has become a puzzle that often leaves a buyer confused. Now there are hundreds of brands on the market, and snowboards are so advanced and complicated and chock full of special features that the choices can be overwhelming.

If you're looking to buy your first board, congratulations! Having your own board is exciting and liberating. It's time to stop wasting money on low-end rentals and invest in something long term that you can call your own. If you've been riding for years but are looking to explore your options, then listen up. Your riding experience may be about to change forever.

Let's start with some background information: Snowboards range anywhere from $250 for a used, generic board to upwards of $1,000 (yes, three zeros) for the latest and coolest creations. You can certainly spend a pretty penny on a board if you want to, but most boards are priced in the middle range between $300 and $500. Plan on spending between $300 and $400 for a well-made board if you are a beginner to intermediate rider, a little more for a more advanced technical deck if you are riding daily and entering the backcountry.

New boards for the current season are most expensive in the fall since they have just hit the shelves and are likely marked full retail. Once Christmas is over and spring hits, board prices tend to drop since retailers are trying to clear their shelves. Sometimes you can get the previous year's deck for a lot cheaper if they are still in stock. Some places will be willing to bargain if it's late in the season because once summer hits, they have little chance of selling them. If you don't need the newest and hottest, opt for a better-quality deck from the previous year. There is rarely a drastic change in technology. Snowboard merchandise is referenced by season. The season runs from fall to spring, so if you buy a board in 2012, it may be labeled 2013 since it is a model made for the 2012-2013 season.

Boards are no longer made just for guys. It wasn't until the late 1990s that board manufacturers really started pushing male- and female-specific models. Although it took some time for all of them to catch on, almost every brand on the market now offers a men's and women's line. All major board manufacturers produce a complete line of men's and women's decks built to suit one's size and riding ability. The basics in board buying depend on your size and weight. The general rule of thumb is the deck should be about as long as your body, as measured from your feet to somewhere between your chin and your nose, depending on the type of riding you plan to do. Snowboards are measured in centimeters, so if you are 5 feet 7 inches (170 cm) tall, for example, you would probably ride a deck in the 150 to 155 cm range.

The size of your foot determines the width of the board you should buy. Many boards offer wide versions for people with bigger feet. When looking to buy, lay the board on the ground and stand on top, preferably with your boots on, with your feet apart, where the holes are drilled for the bindings. Your toes should be close to the edge of the front of the board or hanging over slightly. If they hang over more than an inch (2.5 cm), try a slightly longer deck or a wide version of the board. If your toes hang over the board too much, you will encounter toe drag (your toes will hit the snow when you turn toe-side), which will make it more difficult to ride.

Generally, the more you weigh the stiffer you want the board to be. However, the terrain you plan to ride also factors into the type of board you select. You may want a stiffer deck if you ride hardpack or like to hit the backcountry. We will get into that more in a second. Either way, if you know those two things—the size range and type of deck—the process of purchasing a board will be much easier. The Burton Board Finder on www.burton.com is also an excellent tool to help you find the exact board for you from the get-go.

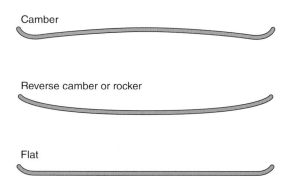

Camber

Reverse camber or rocker

Flat

Each board shape has unique advantages.

Snowboards are categorized as camber, reverse camber (or rocker), and flat. These terms refer to the arch of the deck, since boards are usually arched at different contact points for a range of riding styles. Traditional camber, which is how most boards were originally built, means there is a slight arch in the center of the board and at the tip and tail. This makes for stronger carving and often a stiffer deck. Boards that are built with traditional camber nowadays are freeride or all-mountain specific, meaning they can conquer an array of terrain.

Reverse-camber boards, or rocker decks as they are better known, blew up on the scene and have become most riders' go-to decks. Reverse-camber boards have more rise in the tip and tail and are flat in the center. Although carving responsiveness is compromised on a rocker board, it's easier for the rider to float in powder (i.e., to stay above deep snow instead of sinking) and to maneuver the length of the board. There is less board on the snow, essentially making a rocker the perfect deck to practice spinning and tricks. Rockers are not made for high-speed carving and can get chattery and sketchy when going too fast. Most boards are built reverse nowadays because they are truly easier to ride. They take a lot of the thought out of turning and help catch you when you're falling out of a spin or landing tricks. They are the best decks for beginner and intermediate snowboarders because they are really easy to learn on.

Flat decks are not commonly used or widely available, but they are made by a few brands. Flats are horizontally level, and the tip and tail are only slightly lifted. These decks make for better board feel, meaning you can feel the board connecting with the snow underneath you, and some people just prefer the way a flat deck handles the snow. Flats basically combine a stiffer deck that can handle speed with a board that maneuvers easily in the pipe and on jumps. These decks are not optimal for riding in powder, however.

In the end it's really all a matter of preference. Although your range of options may seem confusing, you'll get to know what you like by testing the boards out. Each brand names these three types of boards (camber, reverse camber, and flat) differently, and each has its own versions. Burton for example labels its reverse-camber decks as rockers and offers different models in which the rocker is spread in different parts of the board. Try one, try them all, switch it up, and you be the judge.

Snowboards are also broken down into three categories: freestyle, freeride, and park. Here's the background on each, and then you can pick your poison.

1. Freestyle. The most popular of all shred stick types, freestyle boards are do-it-all decks that meet the criteria of most riders on the slopes. Freestyle boards are made for riders of all skill levels, from beginner to pro. They are useful for simple carving down corduroy, yet versatile enough for powder and usually the backcountry. Park riding isn't out of the question either. The all-in-one abilities of a freestyle board make learning and improving a breeze. They are generally softer and easier to maneuver all around and are made for less aggressive riders. Freestyle boards are made with more flex and are usually directionally shaped, with either twin tips (the tip and tail are equal

Look for a board designed for your preferred riding style. Shown here are the *(a)* **Burton Custom, a freestyle board;** *(b)* **Burton Fish, a freeride board; and** *(c)* **Burton Blunt, a park board.**

widths) or a smaller nose and wider tail. The stance setting is usually set back or centered (see the section Setting Up Your Board). Freestyle boards enable riders to advance by allowing them the freedom to test different conditions and features without switching decks.

2. **Freeride or big mountain.** These boards are made for more aggressive riders who like to go big and fast. If you like to fly down the hill, yet still feel stable and in control, a freeride deck is perfect for you. Also known as a big mountain deck, a freeride board is unique to its environment. It's important to have a longer deck when taking on big mountains, and freerides are made accordingly. You want to be able to gain speed, and a longer deck means a faster ride. The stiffness helps the rider remain in control while having enough length to float in deep powder. If going out of bounds is in the cards, a freeride is what you need. If you don't have a groomed way down, you don't want to be stuck on a park board or a deck that is too short to maneuver—a stiffer, longer, and bigger deck makes all the difference in this type of situation. Don't compromise on a cheaper board in this case. Freerides are generally more

expensive since they are made with higher-end materials and produced in smaller quantities. If you like to hike or snowmobile to your destination, or if you're lucky enough to take a helicopter ride, you'd better be sure you have a legit freeride board underfoot.

3. **Park.** If playing in the freestyle park and hitting jumps and rails is more your thing, then a park-specific deck is probably best for you. Park boards are made for those who lap the park all day, every day. If you know all you want to do is ride park, you will generally want a smaller board (height to your chin or lower) that is easy to handle. This type of board will make it easier for you to hit the various features and give you more control on rails and jibs. Most park decks are now built with rocker technology, meaning there is a mix of camber and anticamber throughout the board. This makes the board poppier and easy to maneuver on jumps and jibs and smooth on the flats.

Park boards are often twin shaped. Twins are prime for riding switch (with the foot you usually have in the forward position in the rear position and vice versa; see the section Body Awareness in chapter 3 for information on how to determine your natural riding position). Riding switch is key to becoming a versatile, all-around snowboarder. Once you are able to ride both ways, landing tricks—including those triple corks all the kids are doing nowadays—will be a breeze. Maybe. Remember, just because you have a park board and can ride switch doesn't mean you have superpowers!

Bindings

Now that you've got your board on lock, it's time to find the right bindings—the two-part system that holds your feet onto a snowboard. Most bindings offer two straps, one over the toe and the other over the ankle. Bindings have come a long way since the beginning of snowboarding, when boards didn't have them at all. They have helped snowboarders ride bigger mountains and parks faster, stronger, and better.

There have been many innovations in binding tech over the past decade, and it's just as important to understand bindings as it is to know about boards. Although the first systems were just a mechanism to lock your foot down and didn't feature a high-back (the piece behind your ankle and calf), the bindings of today are futuristic and supportive, lending riders the confidence they need to progress the sport. Snap-in or click-in bindings were once thought to be a smart idea, where the bottom of the boot had a metal piece that clicked down to a baseplate, but those fizzled out some time ago because of the minimal ankle support and the danger of the foot coming unlocked.

Although there are many versions on the market today, most bindings are made from plastic or aluminum and feature a highback, baseplate, and two straps. There will be screws and washer hardware for tightening the binding. The baseplate is the circular piece that attaches the binding to the board. The baseplate is where energy is exerted while riding and provides support between boot and board. The plate has numbers that help reference your stance options, so if you want your front foot turned 15 degrees to the right, this piece helps you adjust the position to your liking.

Bindings are sized in small to extra large and are made for both men and women. The size binding you need is determined by your boot size, so bring your boots when you purchase your bindings. Although the two-strap ratchet system is still the

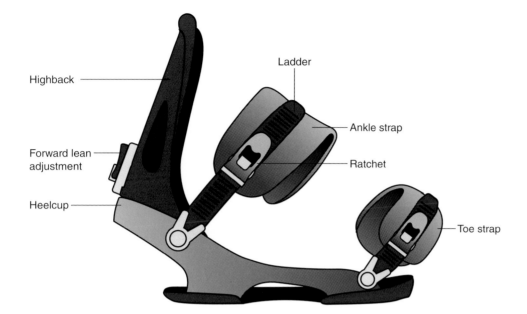

Highback

Forward lean adjustment

Heelcup

Ladder

Ankle strap

Ratchet

Toe strap

Binding components.

most popular, some bindings have one strap that conforms to your boot, making the process of strapping in at the top of the hill quicker and easier. Other bindings offer a back-locking system, in which the highback retracts down and locks in once your foot is secure.

Although the toe strap on most bindings clicks over the top of the foot, some bindings now feature a toepiece where the binding actually pulls your foot back into the bindings. The toepiece also prevents circulation issues since riders tend to ratchet down their bindings too tightly over their toes. You want to make sure your straps are always snug but not overly tight. It's important to be able to feel your feet while you're riding and not be in pain. It shouldn't hurt to make a turn. A good gauge is that when the binding stops clicking, it is tight enough. Don't force the strap one more notch. This can not only cut off circulation but also make the binding unlatch when you're riding, warp the boot, or mess up the ratchet.

As with snowboards, bindings are made for specific types of riding (freestyle and freeride). Freeride bindings are stiffer and built to stabilize your foot in hardpack and big mountain situations. Freestyle bindings are softer and easier to bend, useful for sliding down groomers and hitting park. Of all hard goods, bindings tend to last the longest and are easiest to fix if a piece breaks. How long bindings last depends of course on how much you ride and on their quality. Bindings range anywhere from $75 to $400 and up. A basic but well made binding will run you an average of $200. Something in this price range is a good starting point if you are a casual to advanced rider. More expensive bindings tend to be made with higher-grade plastics and metals, which tend to last longer and perform better. Just like a more expensive car, you get what you pay for most of the time. A higher-end binding is also usually lighter. In snowboarding it's important to not have a ton of extra weight weighing you down. It will just feel bulky and clunky. Plastic is lighter, but some riders prefer metal because it lasts longer and is more indestructible.

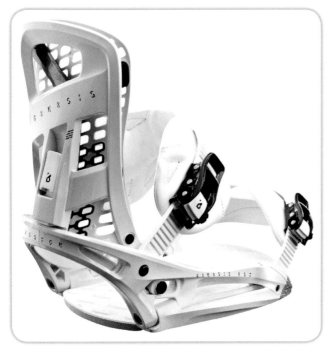

The Burton Genesis, an EST binding for specific boards, makes it easy to adjust your stance.

Some snowboards are built for a specific binding system. This is another reason it's best to first choose a board and then find the right bindings that fit your deck. Burton's Extra Sensory Technology (EST) bindings, for example, are made for their Channel boards. The EST Channel system is a recent innovation that allows the rider to change stance options without unscrewing the entire binding from the board. Simply loosen the screw at the side of the binding and slide the binding up or down the channel until it's sitting where you want it. Systems like this make changing the degree of your foot position a breeze. When it's freezing outside and you want to quickly change your stance, you'll appreciate being able to quickly dial it in instead of having to take your whole deck apart. This is just one way companies are making riding options more simplified and realistic.

On the back of most bindings is an adjustment called forward lean. It helps position your foot forward, making toe-side turns and landings easier. The setting is found on the ankle cup of the binding and is usually adjusted by a plastic piece that is unscrewed and clicked up or down. Bindings with forward lean can have several settings. Most freestyle riders don't use this adjustment very often since it can feel as if your feet and legs are being forced forward. Some do like it for landing tricks, but it just depends on personal preference. As a beginner, consider forward lean at least minimally to help with linking turns. Forward lean is a preference, so if you are unsure, try a few different adjustments to see if it makes a difference for you.

Finding a binding you love is no simple task, so know your options and search with confidence. If you're stuck on traditional bindings there is nothing wrong with that, but don't shut the door on technology. All you should really be concerned about is making sure your foot and ankle are supported and that you feel comfortable. And again remember to check your bindings often to make sure they are tight on the board before you head up the hill. You can usually find snowboard screwdriver tools up on the mountain, but it's not a bad idea to pick up your own minitool that fits right in your pocket in case a situation does arise.

Setting Up Your Board

One of the many reasons snowboards are fun is they can be dialed to your personal specifications. Although someone may have the same snowboard and bindings as you, it's quite impossible for you to have the exact same stance and setup as anyone else. Ski bindings are nearly always mounted in a shop, but snowboard bindings are made to be self-mounted. You are in control of your own destiny when it comes to establishing your stance.

Setup depends mainly on your height and length of deck; however, there are a few other considerations. If you are new to the sport, the first thing you need to do is figure out which way to set up your deck: right or left foot forward. The best approach is to ride a demo setup or take a few lessons beforehand to figure out which way you are most comfortable riding down the hill. (See the section Body Awareness in chapter 3 for more information on how to determine which way you ride.) As you gain experience and want to branch out, you'll find that being able to ride both directions is crucial for dialing in tricks and landing spins.

Once you've figured out which way you ride, lay the board on the ground with the base down, and stand with your feet apart in a comfortable, relaxed way. You can even mess around with having your bindings on the board and get a feel for what it's like to have your boots on too. Generally your feet should be about shoulder-width apart. Both feet should be at an angle, with the front foot facing the tip and the back foot facing the tail at a slight degree. This helps with carving and turning sideways down the hill, since a snowboarder doesn't ride horizontally.

As you get acquainted with your snowboard and become a more advanced rider, you will find that fine-tuning adjustments can do wonders for your progress. As a beginner, it is best to follow basic guidelines with a front-foot angle of plus 20 degrees and a back-foot angle of plus 6. This position allows new riders to force themselves to face one way and hopefully catch on to carving easier. The most common stance is a plus 15, negative 15, which makes for optimal freestyle ability. When both feet are angled, or ducked, the same, it is easier to ride switch and carve at a faster rate.

For the most part, just go with what feels natural when you are standing on the board, and adjust from there. Figuring out what suits you best over time is not only challenging but also part of the fun!

Waxing and Tuning Your Deck

Unless your board has some insane factory wax on the base, you are going to have to tune it up from time to time. Much like a car that needs an oil change every 3,000 miles, your snowboard needs some tender loving care in order to last its lifespan. The better you take care of your deck, the more solid your riding will be overall.

One thing worth mentioning before we get into any of this is rule number one: Always remember to check your equipment before hitting the slopes. Like checking tire pressure and brakes before heading out on a long journey, make sure your boots are laced properly (or locked if you have Boa or some other form of lacing system), and wiggle your bindings to make sure they do not budge. Bindings are the first thing that will come loose after a day of riding and should always be checked before you strap in.

Waxing the Deck

Most boards fresh off the shelves come factory waxed and ready to go. All boards are made with different types of bases, though, which hold or expend wax at different rates. (High-end boards have a better base and hold wax longer.) Most resorts and shops have a station where you can drop your deck off and pick it up freshly waxed and ready to go. The wax on the board takes a beating and needs regular upkeep. You can actually see if your deck's base is dry and even feel the rough texture. The base should feel like a smooth surface.

How long the wax lasts depends on the conditions and the terrain you are riding. On average, you should get your board waxed or wax it yourself every 5 to 10 times you hit the slopes. Over time, the base of your board gets dry because of snow, dirt, debris, and anything you may encounter on the hill. Waxing will help keep your base close to the original (think waxing a car), giving you a more consistent ride and offering better performance overall. In spring, for example, the snow is warmer and your board will often stick to the snow instead of moving right through it. You will feel a stopping sensation in warmer temps if your board has little wax on it because of the variable snow. In winter, when the ground and air are colder, a base will hold wax longer, and sometimes you may find yourself going faster than you would like.

Wax comes in many forms, including a square block, spray-on bottle, or gel. There are also many different types of wax such as all-temp, slush, and X, all-temp being the most popular. All-temp is a basic wax appropriate for variable conditions from winter to spring. Slush wax is used specifically for spring and summer conditions. X, or speed wax, is useful if you're feeling the need for speed.

It's obviously easier to have someone else wax your board for you, but it's also sometimes fun to do it yourself. If you want to do it yourself, make sure you have a garage space or outside area since debris is sure to dirty up the zone. It's also easiest if you have some sort of clamp system and table where the board can lie flat. Companies sell wax tool kits, but a good old fashioned iron also does the trick for application. Just make sure nobody in the house needs to iron clothing with it soon afterward. In fact, you should probably designate an iron for waxing only. Do not use it on clothes once you have waxed a board with one.

Purchase a wax that best meets your needs at a local shop for $5 to $10. Also pick up a base cleaner, and wipe down your board with paper towels or an old rag before applying wax. Just like emptying the old oil out of your car, you want to make sure your base is clean and ready to go before applying wax. Now you're ready to tune her up. Start by heating the iron to a medium temperature. When it's warmed up, carefully hold the iron with one hand and press the wax against the hot surface with the other hand, letting the melted wax drip along the board. Run the iron along the board to spread the wax as evenly as possible across the surface. Allow to dry 30 minutes or so. Using a plastic or metal scraper, scrape off the layer of wax from one end of the board to the other (this is the messy part). You now want to smooth out the base with a tuning brush made to soften the surface. Your base has absorbed the fresh wax and should now look shiny and new.

Maintaining the Edges

You may hear the term *detune* come into play when purchasing a new deck. Since a board usually has super sharp edges off the shelf, many people like to dull the edges because they think sharper edges catch easier. Some boards now come detuned, which means they are already broken in (kind of like a used car), and the way it feels from the get-go is the way the board is going to ride consistently. Like breaking in a new car over its first few thousand miles, boards will get broken in over time, and it can take a few or even 10 rides for you to properly know a board's capabilities.

The metal edges on snowboards do dull over time. Some riders prefer dull edges for boxes and park riding. Sharper edges are key, though, in backcountry, big mountain, and icy situations, and if your edges are dull you will suffer the consequences. Machines in tech shops are your best bet for sharpening edges. Although there are tools to do it yourself, a tech guy will sharpen the edges and give you advice on maintenance.

Accept that wear and tear will occur, and know what to do if you clip your board on a rock or bend an edge. Bases take the most hits, and sometimes you will encounter tree branches and rocks that you may not have time to turn away from. If your base suffers a blow, it can usually be repaired with p-tex, a clear or black stick that can be melted into the base to fill in gashes on a board if it has become damaged. Once again, a tech at a shop can assist with this as well as fix metal edges if they come out of place. He will also let you know if a base is irreparable. To prevent having to buy a whole new expensive deck, try to be aware of your surroundings as much as possible, and keep an eye out for stray branches and rocks. If your board breaks, which is possible, a factory warranty may get you a brand new one depending on when you purchased the board and how the break occurred. Keep your receipt and warranty info somewhere you'll remember in case something happens. Most board brands offer a one- to three-year warranty from the date of purchase.

Take care of your board, as you should maintain your car, and you will find you ride more consistently overall.

Protection

You don't want to be paranoid when it comes to protecting yourself from injury, but you do want to be smart, so give some thought to your protection. Head injuries and broken bones are common among new riders who haven't taken a lesson or who don't know the boundaries of what they are capable of. Consider health insurance to help cover costs, even if it's just for major emergencies. The most common injuries overall are broken arms and wrists, while blowing out a knee is also common for intermediate and advanced riders because of the compression and wear on the joint. Although it is almost impossible for you to prevent something happening to your knee over time, it is quite possible to prevent concussions and breaks.

Helmets

If you purchase only one piece of protection, it should be a helmet. These basic plastic shells protect your most import asset, your brain. Brain injuries and head trauma have become more common as riders have begun attempting more advanced tricks, so wearing one to protect you is a great call. Although a helmet can't completely ensure you won't get a concussion or suffer head trauma, it can provide protection in case you lose control or someone else is booking it right toward you. The thing about protecting yourself is that you never know what other people are going to do. Since there are riders of all abilities on the slopes, it's imperative to be aware of your surroundings at all times.

Helmet protection is pretty basic. Sizing ranges from extra small to extra large, and there are models for men and women. Lots of seasoned riders don't like helmets because they think they aren't cool or think they hinder their riding experience in some way. These are pretty lame excuses when you consider that if you seriously injure your head, there is a high possibility you won't ever snowboard again. Although most helmets were in fact heavy and bulky, the latest and greatest in helmet technology ensures a "you won't even know it's there" feeling.

Try on different models, and figure out your size. Although size can range between brands, find one you like and see how it feels on. The helmet should fit tightly, but not as if it's putting pressure on your head. Shake your head around once you tighten the chin snap, and see if there is any movement. If it slides right off, you obviously need a smaller size. If it feels a little loose, try a size down; if that one feels too tight, the size above it is your best bet. The foam inside the helmet should make it comfortable on your head. Many helmets also have headphones inside so you can easily hook up your MP3 player.

If you hit your head while wearing a helmet, *buy a new one*. Once it's been smashed, even if the helmet doesn't look damaged, suppliers recommend that you replace it. The helmet may have cracked internally, and if you hit your head again, the protection you are counting on may not be there. Although it's true that helmets can't protect you from everything, they can save your life and help prevent or reduce brain damage, so don't take a chance on a potentially damaged helmet.

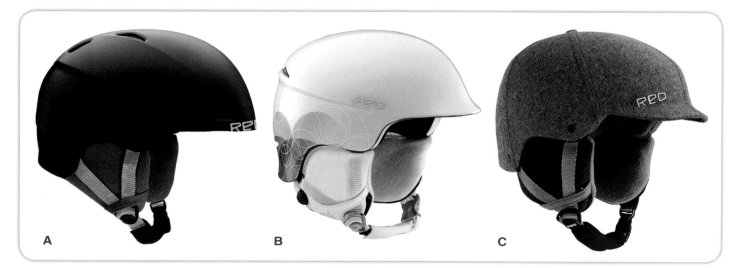

Fit and comfort are key considerations when choosing a helmet, but stylish options are now easy to find.

Goggles

Goggles used to be an afterthought for most companies and even most snowboarders. Goggles weren't "cool," and no one really understood the point of wearing them. The main point is to protect your retinas. The combination of bright sun on white snow is not only glaring and distracting but also extremely harmful to your eyes over time. It is highly possible for your eyes to burn, and you can experience this if you do not take the proper precautions. Sunglasses or any type of ski goggle or dirt-bike face protector used to suffice. Now that riders understand the need for real eye protection, goggles are a must and current models are designed specifically to meet the needs of snowboarders. There are so many brands, frames, and lenses to choose from that finding a pair requires some serious shopping.

Cut the glare and protect your eyes with good quality goggles.

With the right lenses, snowboarding goggles will help you see clearly no matter if it's sunny, the skies are gray, or it's dumping snow. Goggles will also help protect your eyes and face from the elements, including wind and snow. Most goggles are helmet compatible and are made wide through the frame so you can see far at a wide range in both directions. Check the range of your peripheral vision as you test. Brands offer a variety of frame sizes for little tikes to adults. Any given brand has four or more models to make sure each face and head size are covered. There will be an adjustable strap with either a clip or plastic extension to lengthen or tighten the frame around your face. Just as with sunglasses, try on different pairs with a beanie or helmet so you can make sure you are getting the appropriate fit. Make sure there are no gaps underneath your eyes or around your nose. The goggles should be snug but not too tight. You don't want indentation marks left on your face after wearing them.

Polarized lenses, as with sunglasses, offer the best protection. Polarized lenses may or may not change the color of the lens, but they add peace of mind for those with sensitive eyes or those who want to take the best possible care of their eyes. If you are willing to spend a little extra, opt for polarized lenses because they are better quality and provide greater protection. They are the ultimate glare cutters and reflectors, and they let in only a safe and appropriate amount of light.

People tend to get confused when it comes to figuring out which lens color they need. It really depends on where you will be riding the most (see table 2.1). The majority of goggles offer an extra lens, or you can purchase spares if you want variety, which isn't a bad idea. Lenses are generally simple to remove and change out. Just use the goggle wipe that came with the goggles to prevent possible scratching.

One thing to consider is that weather changes rapidly. One minute it might be storming, the next it could be bright blue and sunny out. Check the weather and plan accordingly. Bring a couple of spare goggles or lens colors, if you have them, just in case you need to change them out.

Goggle lenses are very sensitive and prone to scratching. Look for anti-scratch lenses, although even those won't prevent all damage. Take extra care of your goggles. Make sure you always use the soft case when you don't have them on.

TABLE 2.1 LENS COLOR GUIDE

Here is a guide to different lens color options and the conditions they work best in.

Mirrored	Mirrored lenses come in a variety of colors. Mirrored lenses don't necessarily change the color you are looking through; they just block extra light from entering and are good for people with more sensitive eyes. Get a colored lens that is mirrored if you ride where it is mostly sunny and bright out.
Clear	You will rarely ever need this lens, but choose it if you are a night rider. They are also good for super stormy conditions to help you see clearly, although a yellow lens might still be a better option and is more versatile.
Yellow	Lemon-colored lenses are appropriate for overcast and stormy days. If snow is coming down, a yellow lens will make the ground pop so you can actually see where you are going. Yellow really brightens things up and is a good option for those who ride mostly in areas where it snows often or the east coast where gray skies are inevitable.
Pink	Pink lenses are similar to yellow but dilute the contrast a bit. This is a good in between lens if the weather changes from snowy to sunny. It is versatile and ideal in most conditions.
Orange	An orange lens really tones down the brightness on sunny days. This lens is common for those who spend most of their time on sunny slopes.

A problem many riders have with goggles is fogging. If you are a heavy breather and you are wearing a bandana over your mouth, there is a possibility your goggles will fog. Although your body is trying to retain heat, your goggles may hold in moisture, causing fog—much like the inside of a windshield when it's cold outside. If they won't clear up, remove them from your head and air them out. It's a good idea to keep the soft case in a convenient pocket so you can wipe them down as well. If you have persistent problems, it is possible that moisture has entered the lens between the plastic layers. They may take some time to dry out if so, and you may find yourself frustrated. Take a break and let them warm up inside. If they keep fogging, you may need to buy new lenses. Don't buy a whole new set of goggles if you don't need to. Just pick up an extra lens at a nearby shop and replace them.

If you wear glasses, most brands offer a goggle model that will fit over your frames.

Wrist Guards

Wrist guards are helpful when you're a beginner since you will most likely have the tendency to put your hands down to catch yourself. This bending of the wrist over time can cause a sprain or break. One of the first things you should learn as a beginner is to never put your hand down flat if you are falling. Always make a fist and try to land on your forearm, since that part of your arm can handle more compression. If you are still paranoid, pick up some wrist guards for added peace of mind.

A wrist guard slides on your hand and through your thumb. Basically, a hard piece of plastic runs from the middle of your

For those who are learning how to fall safely, wrist guards trump broken wrists.

hand to the middle of the wrist as well as over the top of the hand. It can take a while to get used to wearing wrist guards, but the extra security is worth it. Wrist guards go under your gloves and usually tighten at the top and bottom with Velcro.

Padding

The most common padding is butt pads simply because they cushion the lower back and bottom, which you will often be falling on when you are beginning. It is also something to consider if you have injured your back before or broken your tailbone. Butt pads are worn over your first layer but under your snowboard pants. They are made like shorts, with foam piecing in specific spots.

Other protective snowboard gear includes chest protectors, which act as armor for your upper body to prevent shoulder injuries and back issues. Choose padding for an injured or vulnerable area, or if you're paranoid and fear the worst, choose all and be a true warrior on the slopes.

Worn like a backpack underneath your gear, this back protector provides an extra measure of security.

Soft Goods

What works for you in terms of layering and outerwear depends on your body type and how you react to temperature. If you are a cold-blooded person, figuratively of course, then you need specific layering that is going to hold in warmth all day long. For riders who are always hot, fewer layers but the right layers are best.

Layers

For most snowboarders, less is more when it comes to layering. As mentioned before, one pair of snowboard-specific socks will suffice, and a solid base layer will do for most conditions. There is no need to triple layer, even when it is freezing out. All extra layers will do is make you sweat more, since most first-layer fabrics are designed to retain heat when it's cold and release heat when it's hot. When you sweat and the moisture can't air out, it can actually work against you, and you can end up cold. The number and type of layers depend not only on the way your body holds in heat but also on where you ride. Once you start riding a lot, you will get to know how many layers you need on a day-to-day basis.

Thermals, fleece, and wool are perfect first layers. Cotton is usually a bad call since the fabric isn't as breathable and can more easily get wet. You want a fabric that allows air to flow through. You also want to make sure the first layer on your top and bottom fits tightly against your skin. If they're loose, they won't do much for you. Try on some different options to make sure you are getting the proper fit. Microfleece is a great soft material that feels nice and isn't itchy on your skin. For the top layer, a tank or tee and a long sleeve is a good option. That way you can take off a layer if you need to, or if you take off your jacket you can still be warm enough.

Since you never know what the weather may bring, it's smart to always pack or wear a few extra layers and take some dry socks just in case a situation arises.

Outerwear

Outerwear tech continues to advance year after year. Most companies go to great lengths to test their products, making sure they not only keep you dry but are functional and stylish too. There are a variety of fits to suit any rider's style, from slim to baggy. Most riders choose the loose look since it is comfortable and easy to move around in. But you don't want to feel like a big puffball. Make sure you don't feel either overwhelmed or constricted by your gear. Gear that is too tight can be just as uncomfortable as gear that is too big and baggy.

Outerwear is a way for riders to express their personality. It's cool to make a fashion statement, but on the hill it should be more about function than fashion. Luckily brands nowadays offer an array of highly functional and fashionable gear. Some riders choose to stand out in bright colors and prints, while others prefer all black. The fun part year after year is seeing the new trends and trying on new gear. Even though you may not be able to afford new gear every season, it's still neat to check it all out. Unless you ride 50 or more days a year, your pants and jacket should last three or more seasons. If you are a rider who lives in your outerwear, you may need to purchase a new piece or two each year. Besides general wear and tear, you will be able to tell when your outerwear is failing you when it holds moisture and doesn't dry out.

Outerwear works on a rating system that is measured in millimeters and grams. You will see labels stating different numbers, such as 10000MM/5000G. This means the fabric is 10,000 millimeters waterproof and 5,000 grams breathable. The higher both those ratings are, the more protection you are getting and the better the jacket is. A 10K rating for both waterproofing and breathability is a standard solid rating that you know is going to last for some time. You will see ratings up to 20,000, but past that there is also Gore-Tex, which is said to be the best since there is no rating available. Burton and many other companies carry Gore-Tex products and offer an array of rated jackets to suit your needs. Dryride, made by Burton, is another technology worth mentioning. There are different levels of Dryride, but basically it is another fabric that wicks moisture away and keeps you as dry as possible. You never want to rub your jacket when it has snow or water on it since this can actually make the fabric absorb moisture. It's best to shake or gently push the snow off you if you must.

Most jackets and pants provide a number of added features, from goggle wipes and pockets for MP3 players to plastic holders to prevent your valuables from getting wet. Many jackets also have a powder skirt that can be cinched tight and snaps to the pants, made for keeping snow out when riding powder. Most powder skirts are removable. Puffy jackets are great in extra cold conditions, while shell jackets are best for warmer climates. Ask your salesclerk about all the functions of the gear before choosing your ultimate kit.

Gloves

Gloves are a necessity riders cannot do without. Hands are one of the first things to get cold, and if they aren't warm your whole body can suffer. A good pair of gloves is recommended. Like any other type of outerwear, gloves should be waterproof to help your hands stay dry all day long. Most snowboard-specific gloves are built to repel the elements, so it's more a matter of style and comfort that determines which pair to buy. There are a few different types of gloves, but regular five-finger hand warmers are the most popular. Mittens are also common since they allow your hands to stay warmer and are easier to put on and take off. Spring gloves or inner liners of most gloves are perfect for warmer temps since they are smaller and made with less material. Depending on your riding location, choose a pair of gloves that meets your needs. The basic and most common gloves are made from materials similar to outerwear, but there are leather gloves as well. Some people prefer leather for its durability, but it does tend to get wet more so than a standard glove. Gore-Tex gloves are the best of the best, and if you can afford them they'll be worth the loot.

The inner liner or inside of the glove is usually fuzzy and should feel nice on your hand. You want your fingers to be touching close to the end. Gloves shouldn't be too complicated to get on. If they are, explore other options. Most gloves will have a drawstring, Velcro, or snap so they can tighten over or under your jacket to prevent water and snow from getting inside. Sometimes gloves will even have a small squeegee on one of the fingers to wipe your goggle lens if it gets wet. If you find your hands are still cold time and time again, try putting hand warmers inside. For about a dollar, little hand-warmer packs will ensure your hands stay warm all day.

Once you've found the right setup, you're ready to take it to the slopes. Check out chapter 3 to learn what to expect when you get there.

What to Expect

Many people hesitate or fail to even attempt snowboarding because of the humiliation factor. Putting yourself out there and risking looking like a fool can be intimidating, but knowing what to expect can help tremendously.

The road to becoming an advanced or even a competent rider is rarely a short one, and you are likely to struggle, possibly over and over again. You may feel inept and begin to think you are incapable. Remember that everyone has been there, so don't waste your time and energy worrying about how you look and comparing yourself to others.

Just concentrate on your own skill set, and progress at a speed that is comfortable for you. There is no time limit. There are no extra points for advancing quickly and no penalties for taking it slow. All that matters is that you work toward an understanding of what you are doing and eventually reach the level of snowboarding you want. Trust that it will come. If you don't trust yourself and believe you can do it, you will continue to struggle and fail.

Snowboarding gives back tenfold what you put in. Accept the struggle and acknowledge that the payoff is going to be something you've never experienced before. Look to the end result. Picture yourself standing atop a mountain, captivated by the world that surrounds you, feeling the breeze through your hair and reveling in the accomplishment of having become a snowboarder. Taking part in the sport will make you more self-aware and bring more joy to your daily life.

Once you accept that it will be tough going at first, believe that it's possible, and focus on moving toward your desired goal, whether it's simply to make turns or to get sponsored. There's no rush, so be sure to take it all in at your own pace, but first take some time to watch and learn.

Film Study and Visualization

What should you do first? Watch others. A great way to learn and understand what you are supposed to look like (or not look like) on the board is by studying others.

Magazines and videos are often the teasers that draw people to snowboarding in the first place. The lifestyle and fun depicted in these media outlets inspire people to be a part of it. The rad thing about snowboarding is that it is very much an individual sport, yet it offers many opportunities for camaraderie and friendship. Being able to find a crew and share the mountain with other people who enjoy it as much as you do can make the experience that much better.

Reading up on the sport and watching snowboarding videos before even hitting the mountain will help you grasp the basics of riding down the hill. Although the riders may be doing some gnarly tricks and riding advanced terrain, following their moves will help you ease into the sport and realize what is possible.

Watch everything you can and study it. Take advantage of video sites such as YouTube, Vimeo, and Hulu to view days upon days of snowboarding. This will kick-start the visualization process. Just as it helps to believe you can snowboard, it also helps to picture and imagine yourself doing it. Keep in mind that most videos make snowboarding look like a piece of cake. With dedication and practice, it will be. Start to imagine yourself carving down the mountain. Use the videos as a way to channel energy toward achieving your snowboarding goals. Get excited!

Body Awareness

A snowboarder, like a skateboarder or surfer, is either regular-footed (left foot forward) or goofy-footed (right foot forward). If you have done another board sport, you probably already know which direction you prefer to ride. Precisely where the terms came from is unclear, but it seems likely whoever coined the terms rode left-foot forward and considered the opposite method goofy! Wherever the terms came from, you will be more inclined to ride one way or the other, and as you prepare to hit the slopes, you'll want to have an idea of which is more comfortable for you.

Most rental boards are set up regular, with the left foot in front. If you have no clue by the time you hit the resort, try regular first. The motion should be similar to a skateboarder cruising and gaining speed down a street. If you are feeling as if you aren't getting the hang of it by the middle of the day, switch it up and ride goofy.

The next item on the list is balance. Balance is one of the biggest challenges of learning how to snowboard. You don't need to have the skills of a gymnast or tightrope walker, but having good, general balance and agility will make learning to snowboard that much easier. This doesn't mean that if you don't have good balance you won't be able to snowboard; it just means it might take you a little longer to get the feel of it and catch on. No one is great at everything right away, and those who excel at something are not always those who catch on the fastest.

Think of any sport or physical activity you do well. There's sure to be at least one, whether it's riding a bicycle, sinking a basket, or dancing. You can apply the motor skills, coordination, and body awareness you used in that sport or activity to learning to snowboard. Being confident and aware of what your body can do is a great start. Visualizing a fluid back-and-forth motion and moving your body in an S shape will help make your goal clear. This may sound ridiculous, but it works. Get in the zone and start the process. You won't be bummed you did.

Having a board strapped to both of your feet will likely mess with your head at first. It's hard not to think about the fact that you can't move your legs as you normally would. You will likely feel uncomfortable and restricted in the beginning. If this sounds like torture, don't be alarmed! Snowboarding has its extreme side, and movements on the board have consequences, but the sport wouldn't be as popular as it is if it couldn't be done safely. The challenge is all a part of the fun. Don't let the fear factor discourage you. Be mindful of the consequences of being careless or trying more than you are ready for, but don't let fear take over your head. Remember, you never have to leave the ground if you don't want to.

Having decent balance beforehand will help your cause, but staying agile and flexible as well as practicing balance techniques throughout your snowboarding term will make you a better snowboarder. Being able to balance and catch yourself before you fall is a huge advantage. Many people say if you can ski then you can snowboard. This is far from the truth. If you can ski, then you have been on snow and know what that feels like. But the muscles you use are completely different, and both legs are strapped to one piece of wood instead of two—oh, and you don't use poles.

If you've skateboarded or done another board sport, you will certainly have an advantage because you understand the movements and are used to balancing on a board. Snowboarding uses mainly the lower body, the hips, and the legs, so making sure those are loose and strong will help as well. Do what you can to work on your balance, and you will be a better snowboarder all around.

Yoga is great for strengthening and balance, as are activities such as stand-up paddleboarding and balance boards. See chapter 9 for specific exercises you can do to get your snowboarding muscles toned up.

Know that you are going to fall, but don't let it deter you from trying. Falling is a part of learning. Everyone falls. Even Shaun White still falls. Learning how to fall properly and not seriously injure yourself (see chapter 4) is extremely important, and wearing protective gear (see chapter 2) will help keep you safe.

It's going to take time to get the hang of it. Understand that snowboarding is an investment. Once you've decided to go for it, dedicate your time and energy toward making it a reality. Make sure you have fun. Laugh at yourself. Everyone has been there. It will be easy to get angry and discouraged, but try your hardest to let it go. You're only going to bring other people down if you're in a bad mood. Some riders may get the hang of linking turns their first day, but for most it takes several outings. You will more than likely be able to turn on one edge your first day if you have a good instructor or friend who can properly instruct you. One edge, either the toe side or heel side, will come more naturally. You are going to be taking a lot of baby steps. Enjoy each one of them, and be proud of what you accomplish.

If you have a friend who's been snowboarding for a while and is willing to help you out, ask if he will walk you through the basics. Although taking a class with a certified instructor is a great idea, you may find it less intimidating to go out for your first time with someone you know. If you don't have a friend who can help teach you, take a private lesson or find a class with a group no larger than six people to maximize your learning potential. In a more personal setting, you will get more individual attention and more specific pointers. This will greatly improve your chances of succeeding from the get-go. If you're going to invest the time and spend the money on all the gear, lift tickets, and traveling, don't skimp on the lesson.

Expect some pain. You are going to be sore after your first day, especially if you fall a lot. You are sure to feel muscles ache you never knew you had. Take it easy. Don't try to go all day and push yourself too hard. If you are on a weekend getaway, you might not be able to make it up the next day if you do too much from the start. There's no need to overdo it. No one should be pressuring you to continue if you know you are in true pain. You know your body best, so feel what is going on, and take breaks when you aren't fully up to it. Until your body builds muscle memory, there are sure to be days in the beginning when it will be hard to get out of bed. Hit the hot tub at night or get a massage to alleviate any soreness and help loosen your muscles.

On your first day, *do not* go straight to the chairlift. First learn how to strap on and take off your bindings, and get used to pushing yourself around on the snow at the base of the mountain, in an open space. Stay bent and low. If your legs are straight and locked, you will find it a lot more difficult to move around. If you opt for a class, a good instructor won't take you up until the end of the session when she knows you are capable of riding a lift. This is for your benefit as well as the safety of others.

This is a good time to see if it's easier to push yourself around with your left foot strapped in front or your back. You have only one foot strapped in until you get off the lift at the top.

THE SEVEN TRUTHS OF SNOWBOARDING

Accept these seven statements as fact, and you'll have a better time when you hit the slopes for the first time:

1. You are going to fall. Everyone falls.
2. You are going to feel uncoordinated. Everyone feels uncoordinated when learning something new.
3. Feeling embarrassed is optional and will not improve your performance.
4. Visualizing helps. So does trusting your body.
5. You may love or hate snowboarding right away. Either way, you'll get better with practice.
6. You are going to be sore by the end of the day.
7. If you are optimistic and focus on having fun, you will enjoy the ride.

Having a snowboard strapped onto your foot takes some getting used to. Try pushing yourself around with the left foot strapped in first. Basically you want to push with your back foot in front of the toe side of the board. If it feels completely awkward and as if you have no control, try strapping the right foot in the front and pushing with your left. This should help you get a sense of what's more natural for you.

Chairlift Navigation

Once you get a feel for moving around on a snowboard in open space on flat terrain, you can head for the chairlift. Chairlifts, open lifts usually with a lap bar, are the most common type of transportation for snowboarders. Most are made for two to four people, but some chairs can ride up to eight. Chairs are the most efficient way to get the most people up the mountain in the shortest period of time. You will find chairlifts at any resort you ride, and you should learn to use them before trying any other type of lift, apart from the Magic Carpet.

You may have to slowly push yourself and wait if there is a line. Pay attention to the riders waiting in line to get on, and watch them as they prepare to board. Before you enter the line, find an area that is clear, and buckle your front foot in. Then you can slide yourself up to the machine or the person will physically scan your pass or ticket before you can proceed. Once you're good to go, continue pushing yourself. If it's not crowded, you don't have to worry too much, but if it's packed, it's good etiquette to group yourself up with others. Lift operators often put people together on a chair, so be prepared to make new friends and strike up a conversation if the opportunity arises. For group riding, goofy riders should ride on the left side of the chair, and

Chairlifts are the most common type of lifts you will encounter. Chairlift etiquette calls for getting on and off quickly and safely. Being friendly is a plus.

regular riders should ride on the right. This prevents possible crossing of the boards on the lift and is a good safety measure.

As the chair swings around and the group or person in front of you gets on, move forward up to the marked line. The tip or middle of the board should be on the line. Don't stand perpendicular to the marked line. Stand facing uphill with the nose of your board pointed toward the top of the mountain. Glance behind you to watch the chair as it comes toward you, then sit down and slide back in the seat. Pull the lap bar down for safety, and keep the front of the snowboard lifted so it doesn't catch in the snow. You should now be sitting comfortably and be heading up the mountain. Most riders set the back of the board perpendicular on their opposite toe to release some of the weight from the front leg. This also makes the ride more comfortable.

Hold on to your personal belongings while on the chair, and carefully adjust your gear or finish suiting up if needed. As you approach the top of the hill, lift the bar and prepare to get off. Turn with your body facing uphill and your front foot forward. As your board touches the snow, use the back of the chair to lift yourself off. Place your loose foot next to the opposite binding, or on a stomp pad (a piece of plastic or material fixed next to your binding) if you have one, to prevent your foot from sliding on the slippery topsheet, and ride away, keeping your knees bent and staying low. The terrain should be flat at the top, so edge your way by skating, as you have practiced out in the open, toward a bench or area where you have enough room to strap your other foot in. Until you are used to lifting yourself off of the ground with both feet strapped in, use a bench if there is one. Sit down and lock your other foot in securely. This is the time to make sure everything else is secure as well: zippers zipped, gloves on, and both boots and bindings tightened. All that's left to do is to get down the hill. That shouldn't be too hard.

Here are other types of lifts you may encounter:

- **Magic Carpet.** This is a surface lift used mainly in beginner areas of a resort. This type of lift is a slow-moving conveyor belt that makes going short distances a breeze. You can ride with one or both feet strapped in because you stand on the "carpet" all the way up. A Magic Carpet is typically situated at the base area of resorts in an enclosed area set up for first-time riders. The Magic Carpet makes getting up the hill quicker, and it's a good lift to get used to before you head for the chairs.

- **Gondola.** A gondola is an enclosed cabin. Boards are not strapped on; riders sit or stand during the ride, and the boards are placed on outside racks or brought inside. Gondolas can hold anywhere from one to dozens of people depending on the size. There are usually seats inside, and they are a much warmer alternative to regular chairlifts in frigid temperatures. The gondola is an enclosed, relaxing transporter, as opposed to open chairs in which you are exposed to the elements. Gondolas are great for going longer distances (sometimes all the way to the top of the mountain) and being able to pack people in safely to the top.

- **Tram.** These large aerial lifts take groups of riders up the hill at one time. You will still find these at esteemed and world-renowned resorts including Jackson Hole in Wyoming, Snowbird in Utah, and Squaw Valley in Tahoe. Trams are often the centerpiece of the resort. They run about every 15 to 30 minutes since the cables can usually hold only two at a time, but they can carry upwards of 50 passengers at once. Most trams have sitting and standing room. Snowboarders don't strap on their boards while riding trams; riders bring their boards inside and hold them until they get off at the top.

The legendary tram in Squaw Valley, California, offers riders a stellar view of the area.

○ **T-bar.** A T-bar is a surface lift where the rider is in contact with the snow the entire ride. You can ride with one or both feet strapped in, depending on what the operator suggests. The rider stays standing and holds onto the center bar while the T of the bar goes behind the rider, pushing the rider up the hill. It can hold up to two riders. When riding, make sure your nose is facing uphill. Don't turn your board sideways.

The bar is shaped like an upside-down T and is made out of metal or plastic. T-bars are an older style of lift, still commonly used at resorts to get to terrain where a full lift could not be installed. T-bars are not comfortable or easy to ride. It takes real concentration and skill to hold on and get to the top. However, they will help you access some great terrain. If you let go, or if your hand slips off, you will be able to ride right away from the bar because it is made to swing up out of the way once the rider lets go.

○ **J-bar.** Similar to T-bars, J-bars are long J-shaped metal lifts made for a single person at a time. Simply lean back, putting your weight onto the bar, and keep your board sliding on the snow smoothly while you hold on. Again, you can ride with one or both feet strapped in depending on what the operator suggests. The J-bar has almost all the same functions as the T-bar, except it's made for a single rider.

○ **Tow rope.** One of the first types of lifts used to help skiers up the mountain, tow ropes are few and far between now, but you may occasionally find one. Simply hold onto the rope with both feet strapped in and be pulled up the hill. There will be a ball-like plastic object or something similar to hold on to. Your feet will be on the ground the entire ride, and you'll need to keep your nose facing uphill. Tow ropes are similar to a large pulley and are generally made for going short distances. It can take only one rider at a time, unless otherwise permitted. The tow rope is a slow-moving lift, but it gets the job done if you aren't up for hiking.

Altitude Adjustment

If you aren't used to being at high elevations, acclimating yourself to the change in altitude may take some time. It's not uncommon to experience a light-headed dizzy sensation if you don't spend much time in the mountains. Basically as you travel higher in elevation, there is less air pressure and the air becomes thinner. This means the cells in your body have to work harder to transport enough oxygen to your lungs and brain. It takes time, sometimes several days, for the body to adjust. If you travel from sea level or a low elevation, where the air pressure is greater, to higher elevations at a quick rate, you may feel ill as your body attempts to adapt to the new conditions.

At sea level or low altitudes, it is easy to breathe and do regular activities. As you climb in elevation, there is less air pressure and it becomes harder to breathe, especially when exerting yourself. If you are not acclimated and prepared for this change, you may start to feel out of it and light-headed. Airplanes are pressurized as they climb upward so passengers experience only minimal effects from the increase in elevation. Even if you are acclimated in the airplane (if that is how you traveled), once you land at your destination, you may still get woozy.

TABLE 3.1 RESORT ELEVATION CHART

Resort and location	Base elevation	Summit elevation
Breckenridge, Colorado	9,600 ft (2,926 m)	12,840 ft (3,914 m)
Taos, New Mexico	9,237 ft (2,815 m)	12,481 ft (3,804 m)
Crested Butte, Colorado	9,375 ft (2,858 m)	12,162 ft (3,707 m)
Vail, Colorado	8,120 ft (2,475 m)	11,570 ft (3,527 m)
Aspen, Colorado	7,945 ft (2,422 m)	11,212 ft (3,417 m)
Mammoth Mountain, California	7,953 ft (2,424 m)	11,053 ft (3,369 m)
Jackson Hole, Wyoming	6,311 ft (1,924 m)	10,450 ft (3,185 m)
Heavenly, Nevada	6,565 ft (2,001 m)	10,067 ft (3,068 m)
Squaw Valley, California	6,200 ft (1,890 m)	9,050 ft (2,758 m)
Sun Valley, Idaho	5,920 ft (1,804 m)	9,020 ft (2,749 m)
Big Bear, California	7,140 ft (2,176 m)	8,805 ft (2,684 m)
Northstar Resort, California	6,330 ft (1,929 m)	8,610 ft (2,624 m)
Whistler/Blackcomb, Canada	2,214 ft (675 m)	7,494 ft (2,284 m)
Mt. Hood Meadows, Oregon	5,250 ft (1,600 m)	7,300 ft (2,225 m)
Whitefish, Montana	3,028 ft (923 m)	6,817 ft (2,078 m)
Steven's Pass, Washington	4,056 ft (1,236 m)	5,845 ft (1,782 m)
Mt. Baker, Washington	3,500 ft (1,067 m)	5,089 ft (1,551 m)
Killington, Vermont	1,165 ft (355 m)	4,241 ft (1,293 m)
Stratton, Vermont	1,872 ft (571 m)	3,874 ft (1,181 m)
Loon, New Hampshire	950 ft (290 m)	3,050 ft (930 m)

The decrease in air pressure can cause altitude sickness or acute mountain sickness. It's not completely possible to prevent or eliminate altitude sickness; even people who live in the mountains can experience it from time to time. But there are a few things you can do to help your body adjust. You don't want altitude sickness to ruin your trip.

The higher you are going, the more difficult it can be to adjust—going up 10,000 feet (3,000 m) from sea level can have a greater impact on you than traveling a few thousand feet, although any significant change in altitude can produce physical symptoms. Table 3.1, which lists the base and summit elevations at some popular resorts, will give you a good idea of how high up you will be in relation to what you are used to. Whose job it was to measure it is an interesting question, but it is helpful to compare the heights of the mountains. As you can see, resorts on the west coast are much higher than those on the east. A higher elevation doesn't necessarily mean steeper terrain, but if you were to travel from sea level (0 feet) to a height upwards of 12,000 feet (3,700 m) in a short time, your body would have some serious adjusting to do.

There are a few simple steps you can take to adapt more easily to the change in elevation: Stay hydrated, rest, and supplement your oxygen intake.

1. **Stay hydrated.** Drinking tons of water is the key to keeping yourself from feeling sick or out of it. You may notice within minutes of being in the mountains that your skin and lips are dry. This is because the air in the mountains is dry, and the moisture from your skin is trying to hold onto what it has.

You should hydrate as much as possible with plain water to gain some moisture back and help you stay charged. Drink more than you think you need to. Drink plenty of water in the days leading up to the trip, and then continue drinking more than the daily recommended number of glasses every day you are in the mountains. Dehydration is the number one factor in getting sick.

2. **Rest.** Getting good rest before your trip will greatly help you adjust to the altitude. A well-rested body performs better and has more energy throughout the day. Snowboarding takes a lot of effort, and if you're not used to all the work it takes to gear up and ride all day, then you are going to be miserable. Do yourself a favor and sleep. It's also not a bad idea to give your body a rest after a day on the hill, either. Your body has been working hard, so take some time to relax and lie down, then hit the hot tub and grab an ice-cold beverage to celebrate your day.

3. **Use oxygen.** It's not completely necessary, but breathing oxygen from an oxygen cylinder can make adjusting to the altitude easier. Climbers and hikers use oxygen cylinders, since ascending at a fast rate at such a high altitude can make them light-headed and feel as if their lungs are in pain. Losing oxygen and lung capacity when you go up in elevation can cause you to lose oxygen to your brain, which is what causes some climbing deaths. Although it is highly unlikely you will die on a snowboarding trip to the mountains, be aware that you may experience some form of altitude sickness and that oxygen cylinders can help prevent it or reduce its severity. Cylinders quickly put oxygen back into your lungs. Use them as soon as you get to your destination and throughout your trip if necessary. A cylinder is made to be used only a few times, so you will need refills if you are going to use it more than that. Pick one up at an REI or an outdoor store. You can also rent cylinders at participating stores and resorts, and employees there can discuss the options with you and explain the protocol for using one. You can use them inside or outside, but it's best to use them right before you are going out to ride.

Resort Amenities and Safety Precautions

Most resorts are built with the customer experience in mind, yet some resorts are much more lavish than others. Always research beforehand so you know what to expect as far as lodging, amenities, shops, dining, and the surrounding area. Some bigger resorts have on-mountain lodging so you don't have to travel all the way down to the base or to town (if there even is one) to eat.

Shuttle service to and from town and lodging is also available at many resorts. If you can save yourself the drive and the parking fee and reduce your footprint on the environment, you should opt to do so. Many shuttle services are complimentary. Make sure you note your stops and know how to get to and from your destination.

There should be plenty of restroom facilities and water sources on the mountain, and you will surely get thirsty. The elevation and dry climate make you extra dehydrated, so keep this in mind and drink lots of water, even when you don't feel thirsty.

Many resorts are located in remote locations where Internet and cell service can be sparse. Know this from the get-go and arrange meeting locations and backup plans in case you lose the people you are with.

If you are riding a mountain you are unfamiliar with, always carry a trail map and follow signs. U.S. resorts are required to have mountain safety employees who ride around and make sure everyone is being safe, going slowly in slow zones, and following the rules. Don't be afraid to ask questions or for directions if you are lost. Ski (or snowboard) patrollers, wearing red jackets with a medical cross symbol, should be nearby in case an accident occurs. If for some reason you are unable to ride or get down the mountain, call out to someone to get you a patroller. It is always a good idea to ride with a partner. If something does happen, you will have someone looking out for you. Especially when you are a beginner, ride with a buddy or group so you can keep an eye on each other.

Patrollers work hard to keep the terrain in good shape and the riders safe. They are first on the mountain every morning, setting up barriers and scanning runs to make sure there is nothing on the trails that can easily injure a rider. These CPR-certified on-mountain medics are skilled skiers and riders. They have been well trained to provide efficient and proper safety service for riders on the mountain. If someone is unable to make it down the mountain because of an injury or other emergency, the patrollers make sure the rider is taken down safely on a flat stretcher and brought to the medical facility at the resort. Resort doctors and medical centers do not perform surgeries, but they are helpful for minor injuries, and in the event of severe injuries, they provide care until the ambulance or helicopter can take the injured rider to a hospital.

Every resort has an emergency number guests can call. Keep it with you so you can call for help in the event that you or someone you encounter needs assistance.

Although you want to minimize the amount of stuff you carry with you in a pack or pockets while snowboarding, make sure to hold on to these few necessities:

- A cell phone with the resort emergency number programmed. Protect it in a pocket with a cloth or case, and keep it somewhere it won't hinder your ability to strap in or ride.
- Identification. Keep a license or some form of identification on you at all times.
- Ticket or pass. Most jackets have a "pass pocket" where you can store your pass. Some machines can scan your pass or magnetic card right through your jacket so you don't even need to take it out. A ticket, on the other hand, should be hooked on the pants or jacket with a metal or plastic piece provided at the ticket window; it should be hooked preferably on your front-foot side so it can be viewed and scanned easily by ticket scanners.
- Lip balm. Prevent windburn and dry lips by keeping a tube of lip balm handy. Any skin that is exposed to the elements will dry out, so stay moisturized with a good tube of lip balm.
- A little cash or credit. Always carry some money in case you get hungry or need to purchase something on the mountain you forgot. Place it somewhere it won't fall out, with your ID.

Know the rules and follow them. There's no need to be paranoid, but be aware of everything that is going on around you, and do all you can to keep yourself and other riders safe.

As you get off the lift, use the look-before-you-leap technique. Get yourself in order, and make sure there is enough room in front of and around you to head down the hill. Avoid crowds of people standing or sitting on the hill. If you ride regular, it's a good idea to stay on the left side of the run so as to avoid anyone coming up behind you, in your blind spot. If you ride goofy, stay on the right side of the run to avoid colliding with someone who may not see you.

If you are coming up on a slow rider and can't tell which direction he is going to go, slow down. Don't startle the rider by flying by without warning. Slow down immediately, and if possible, announce that you want to pass. Try to give the rider space, and ride far on one side or the other until you have passed. Don't try to guess which way a skier or boarder is going. Ride as far out of the way as you can, and slow down to prevent a collision. Know that the person in front of you has the right of way.

There are merging trails on mountains where riders converge from all different directions. Look uphill and know your surroundings. Slow down, and if it looks clear, proceed. As with a yield sign when driving a car, the protocol is to look first and then proceed.

If you fall or if someone is coming up on you fast, wait for others to pass. Stay put until you are sure it is safe to get up and continue. Remember, the person in front has the right of way, but if you are able to see what is going on uphill, it will only make you a safer rider. Although you can't always prevent someone from crashing into you, try to be as aware as you can of other riders near you. It's all about prevention. The more you can prevent something bad from going wrong, the more fun you will have and the safer a rider you will be.

Weather

Staying on top of what the conditions will be like when planning a trip to the mountains is important. Knowing what type of conditions to expect and preparing accordingly is sure to make your trip more relaxing and enjoyable. An informative website for specific and precise weather conditions is www.noaa.gov. Simply enter the town and state, and target the area where you are heading. You can find out not only whether there is snow in the forecast but also just how likely it is and how much is expected in specific time frames. Checking the weather also helps you pack and put on the most appropriate clothing options.

As you snowboard more often and improve your skills, you'll find that monitoring the weather becomes an integral tool in determining what gear and type of board to bring, if you have more than one. It also becomes crucial for hitting the right mountains and understanding conditions in the backcountry.

Although it helps to know what kind of weather is likely to be in store for you, keep in mind that weather can be unpredictable and changeable. In the mountains, weather can change drastically in a short period of time. Be prepared for sudden changes by layering up and letting someone know where you are headed. If you plan to drive, keep plenty of gas in your vehicle, and bring blankets, food, water, and flares in case a storm rolls in and you get stuck somewhere.

Do your best to plan ahead, but don't forget to get stoked! Although there is a lot to learn and it can take a good amount of time and energy just to *get* to the mountain, the payoff is undeniable. Be open to the experience, believe in yourself, pay attention to your surroundings, and you will do just fine.

You are now ready to venture down the mountain!

Basic Techniques

Now that you understand what snowboarding is about and you have your equipment, it's time to get the party started. Part II starts with instructions on all the basics, from standing up to linking toe-side and heel-side turns.

In chapter 5 we'll fill you in on the rules of snowboarding and what not to do on the slopes. We'll explain the responsibility code, general rules of riding on the mountain, and the Smart Style terrain park code. We'll help you learn to be in control and stay in control.

In chapter 6 we'll break down the signage at resorts and talk about the types of terrain you can expect. We'll also help you get educated about riding out of bounds and spell out the precautions you should take before doing so. Finally, we'll help get you ready to ride everything: jumps, jibs, the halfpipe, and natural features. It's go time!

Getting Started

There's no doubt you will feel a mix of emotions when heading up to the hill to snowboard for your first time. Excited, scared, nervous—these are all common feelings for beginners and even veterans. Part of the excitement of snowboarding is the adrenaline and anticipation of what is going to happen. Some people are naturally anxious, and this may make the thought of snowboarding nerve-racking.

Calm your nerves by getting a good night's rest, eating a healthy breakfast, and always drinking plenty of water. These things will help you feel on your A game and ready for a day on the slopes. Being well rested and having fueled your body will also help give you confidence and longevity.

Many riders like to do some light stretching or even a yoga session in the morning to warm the muscles and to relax and calm the mind. Staying loose and light on your feet is a major part of becoming a great snowboarder. If you are tense and stiff, you are surely going to have a difficult time learning and getting better. Make sure your body is warmed up before you stretch, and don't overdo it. Too much stretching may make you think you can do more than your body is actually ready for. See chapter 9 for more information on stretching.

The more uptight and on edge you are when going up to the hill, the more prone to injuries you will be, so relax. Get focused and remember to breathe. You are about to have the time of your life!

LOOSENING UP BEFORE SNOWBOARDING

If you don't have a lot of time to get loose, perform a 5-minute warm-up by jogging in place or doing some jumping jacks, then lie down on the ground before you boot up and do this quick exercise. Flex your feet and stretch your arms as long as you can above your head. Hold this position for at least 30 seconds. Next, pull one knee toward your belly, lock your hands together, and pull your leg with the knee bent to your chest. Cross your bent knee over your body to help relieve tension in the hips and stretch your back. Use your opposite hand to guide your knee as close to the floor as possible. Now pull your bent knee toward the floor on the other side with the same arm as the bent leg. Return to the starting position, and repeat with the other leg. Do each knee once or twice for 10 to 15 seconds in each position for optimal stretching. If you don't have a nice flat surface to lie on, you can perform this same exercise standing up. You won't get the exact benefits, but you will still feel the stretch.

Another good stretch is to bring your leg up in front and place it on some form of bar or elevated surface. With one leg at a time, try to reach your toes, elongating your back and neck. Do each leg for 10 to 15 seconds. Next put both hands behind your back, interlocking your fingers, and pull your shoulder blades together. Look up to the sky and feel your back stretch. After you're finished, bend your right knee, bringing your heel to your bum and using your right hand to pull your leg back. Do each leg for another 5 to 10 seconds. Now you should be feeling loose and ready to climb mountains.

Don't put pressure on yourself. You should be snowboarding because you want to, not because you think you have to. Especially in the beginning, your only goal should be to learn and have fun. Don't think about what everyone else is doing. Concentrate on your own feats, and don't get flustered or try to force it if you are having trouble grasping a concept. Move on or take a break, and come back to it when you are in a calmer and more positive state.

There is a lot to get used to when you first hit the slopes. Just try to take it one step at a time. You not only have on more clothes than you would usually wear, you are dealing with a lot of relatively unfamiliar equipment as well. Take some time to get used to it. If you don't feel comfortable in your gear, it's going to be difficult from the start to even begin standing up on a board and turning down a mountain. Make sure you are as comfortable as possible in your gear, especially your boots, before you begin. Trying on your getup at home is a good idea and will also get you excited to shred. If you have new boots, they may be stiff and take a while to break in, as mentioned in chapter 2. Be prepared to take it easy if they're hurting your feet—you don't want to push yourself and get frustrated right off the bat. It's okay to take breaks and not go all day if you are distracted by any pain.

Next, double- and then triple-check that all your equipment is securely fastened and ready to use. Nothing should wiggle or feel loose. Don't psych yourself out, though, and don't look for excuses to avoid getting out there. If you're feeling pretty comfortable overall, then it's time to hit the slopes and give it a go.

Manage Your Expectations

Understand that you are going to go fast once you get on the hill—sometimes a lot faster than you would like to go. Later on you will look back and realize it wasn't fast at all, but in the beginning it will seem fast and you will feel out of control, so prepare yourself for that feeling. Learning to stay in control is a major part of snowboarding, especially when there are other people and obstacles on the hill. The last thing you want to worry about is crashing into another person. You are going to want to practice in as wide open a space as possible. Find a place where there is room and a minimal slope. There are designated beginner areas at resorts, so look for those and start practicing. Don't try to look cool and head straight for the lift to the highest peak. You don't have anything to prove to anyone (and you aren't likely to look very cool for long if you try to do more than you are ready for). Be smart and have patience.

Accept that you aren't going to be an instant pro. As with any sport, it takes a ton of time and practice to ride properly and confidently. Once you accept that you are going to take some falls and are going to struggle for a few days (maybe even weeks) your riding is sure to benefit. You must accept that you are going to fall. It's part of the learning process. There's no way around it. Once you accept that falling is unavoidable, you can concentrate on how to properly fall to help prevent serious injury.

Taking a few lessons and using falling techniques such as putting your forearms down instead of your wrists will definitely help. Bending your knees and staying low keeps you balanced and brings you closer to the ground before impact. Try to stay as calm and relaxed as possible. Although it's hard to know how you are going to land, once you begin to fall, try to assess whether you are falling backward or forward, and prepare your body as best you can. If you are falling backward, try to land on your rear end and protect your head by tucking your upper body. If you know what to do from the start, you'll have more confidence. It's like test day at school. If you've been studying and know the material, you'll have a better success rate. If you go in unprepared, you are more likely to fail. Nothing but snowboarding itself can help you *fully* grasp the concept of snowboarding and what it's like to physically do the activity, but learning what you can ahead of time will better prepare you for the experience and help you understand the movements. See the Taking Lessons section later in this chapter for information on what to expect.

Stay Positive

It's easy to get down on yourself when you first start snowboarding, but always remember *everyone* has been there. If you want to succeed you are going to have to stay positive and continue trying. Don't let other people or surrounding circumstances interfere with your learning abilities. Keep in mind that every rider learns at a different pace, and cut yourself some slack.

Having support is always good. Practicing with a friend who has been snowboarding for some time and can offer tips, or even with a buddy who is also just beginning to learn, may make your experience more pleasurable. Sometimes this can backfire, though, if you constantly measure your skills and your progress against your friend's. Professional instruction from people who know how to teach as well as how to snowboard can also be helpful. Figure out what works best for you, whether it's learning one on one with a friend, taking a group lesson, or splurging for a private lesson by a certified instructor.

Relax. It's easy to get frustrated and angry when you keep falling. Remember those seven truths of snowboarding from chapter 3? Take your time, and if you're feeling tired or overwhelmed, take a break. Just don't use breaks as excuses for not continuing to try. Don't be too hard on yourself. Be proud of the baby steps you are taking, and honor yourself for what you are accomplishing. Just getting out there and trying makes you one tough person. Look at what you have accomplished, not what you haven't. It's the glass half full way of thinking. What matters from the start is that you believe in yourself. You've got this! It won't be long before others are asking you to teach them.

Practice makes perfect. And it's going to take a lot of it. Be willing to put in plenty of time. If you don't get a new concept right away, dedicate some hours and see what happens. Don't think of learning snowboarding skills in a predetermined pattern and time frame. It may take one day to feel as if you know what you're doing, or it may take a whole season. You would be amazed by how many people say that one day it just clicked. Anticipate that one day when the pieces will fall into place, and feed off that energy; use it to keep pushing yourself to get up and try again.

The best way to improve is to continue to get out there and conquer your fears. Professional snowboarders have put in years of time, energy, and focus in order to get where they are. If you live near the mountains and you want to see results sooner rather than later, dedicate at least a few days a week to getting on the mountain and simply practicing. If you don't live near the mountains and you want to get better, practice skateboarding and other board activities to hone your balance and coordination so that when you do get to the hill, you will be feeling ready. Practice always makes perfect—eventually.

Standing Up and Staying Up

One of the initial achievements in snowboarding is standing up . . . and staying up. You will notice most beginners and even advanced riders sitting down at the top of the hill, tightening their bindings, and standing up from there. First get a feel for what it's like to be standing with your feet locked in on a flat surface. Keep your entire body and board facing the bottom of the hill at first. If you turn both your body and board sideways, facing the left or right side of the mountain, you will start to move unless you are on flat ground. Look down toward the bottom of the hill because you must always be aware of what is in front of you. This is your responsibility to the other riders on the mountain. It's technically your fault if you hit someone and you were above them. Remember to always maintain as much control as possible, and be aware of your surroundings.

Most riders may feel fine standing on flat ground, and only after they fall down do they realize how hard it is to get back up. When you fall there are essentially two ways to get back up. One is by sitting with your feet in front of you, with your body open and facing downhill. Place both hands behind your body, and use your arms to push yourself up from there (figure 4.1). Bend your knees and stay low so you don't fall forward. Keeping your knees bent and staying low to the ground and centered helps tremendously with all aspects of snowboarding. Riders tend to lock their knees out of habit and nervousness, but locking your knees will only make you fall back down.

The other way to get up is to flip around on your belly, so that your legs are downhill and your body is uphill (figure 4.2). Move onto your knees after you have flipped around so that your body is upright and your knees are bent underneath you with the base of your board facing downhill. Using the ground, put your hands in front of you

FIGURE 4.1   THE SIT AND PUSH METHOD OF GETTING UP.

FIGURE 4.2 THE FLIP ON YOUR BELLY METHOD OF GETTING UP.

and push yourself up to a standing position This way is generally easier once you're already part of the way down the hill and are on more of a slope.. However, some riders like to flip over to get up no matter what. If you can't get up by facing downhill first, try the uphill technique. Your level of flexibility and agility helps determine which method is easier. You will be getting up and down a lot, so knowing what works best for you will help. Most resorts have benches at the top of the lift for you to push to and sit on, strap in, and get up from.

Now *staying* standing is a whole other story. Once you are up, as mentioned before, it is important to stay low and centered, with your knees bent. Facing horizontally, either downhill or uphill, will be a lesson in balance and edge control as explained in the next section.

Balancing Your Body

Snowboarding is all about balance. Now you don't need to have perfect balance, but an understanding of weight distribution and how to use it for board control will make you a better rider. Snowboarding is a lot of leaning back and forth, moving side to side, and turning uphill and then downhill. It's almost impossible to train for balancing and maneuvering on a snowboard without actually doing it. There's nothing else like it. The best way to prepare to balance on a snowboard is to practice on a balance board and do other board sports.

While you're on the snowboard, the best thing to do is tune in to your body and trust it to move as it needs to, in a smooth, balanced, loose, and easy manner. The worst thing to do is stiffen up and resist.

You may have already noticed a recurring theme, and you are sure to hear it over and over again: *Bend your knees!* Watch any accomplished snowboarder, and pay attention to his knees. Veteran riders always keep a low center of gravity. When you learn to keep your knees bent, *always* bent, your riding will improve immensely. It will be easier to balance, turn, and stop. It will be easier to learn and land tricks. Compared with every other factor in the equation of learning how to snowboard, keeping your knees bent is by the far the greatest contributor in helping you succeed.

You want to maintain a comfortable stance, with both your feet at least shoulder-distance apart and angled out. If you are set up in this position, it is practically impossible to not bend your knees. It may feel awkward at first, but try to make it natural instead of forced. Don't overexaggerate this position by bringing your butt below your knees. A lot of people tend to bend all the way down to the ground because they've been told to bend their knees, but a really deep bend won't help you stay balanced. Again, look at the experienced riders. Basically you want a slight bend at the knees, with your hips pulled down and your bum pushed slightly out (figure 4.3). If you remember only one thing when attempting snowboarding, remember to bend your knees.

FIGURE 4.3 THE BALANCED STANCE: KNEES ARE BENT, FEET ARE SHOULDER-WIDTH APART, TOES ARE ANGLED OUT, HIPS ARE DOWN, AND BUM IS SLIGHTLY PUSHED OUT.

It may seem ridiculous, but pushing your hips back and sticking your butt out can help with your balance and technique. Be sure not to completely arch your back because this may actually cause injury. There's no need to exaggerate this movement; it can be subtle and still do the trick. Golfers are great examples of the "stick your butt out" technique. Although they may look silly, this posture can really help improve their swing and ability to drive the ball. On a snowboard, sticking your butt out will at first simply help with keeping your center of gravity low and keeping your knees bent. As you progress, remembering to stick your butt out will help you stay balanced and get the hang of turning and other basic moves. As you become accustomed to riding, you will learn to do this subtly and your posture will look more natural.

Stopping

Understandably enough, one of the first things people want to know when they're learning how to snowboard is how to stop. First of all, it's not by sliding and sitting (or maybe slamming) on the ground. Stopping is a *motion* controlled by the heel- or toe-side edge of your board. Just as with getting up, there are two ways to stop. The easiest way to learn the first method is by doing it. Begin by standing on a gradual or beginner slope with your entire body facing downhill and your board across the incline. Stand with your knees bent, and stay low. Don't think about trying to turn yet. Concentrate on what edge control and stopping feel like. If you're standing on a slope, you will immediately begin sliding down the hill. Think about pressing your heels into the back of the board and lifting your toes very steadily off the ground. People always mess this up and completely flex the foot. It isn't about flexing; it's about pressing. Your board will be doing a lot of the work, but always remember you are the one in control. Now practice sliding downhill while remaining in that position, with your whole body and board perpendicular. Pressing your heels hard into the snow is what is going to make you stop. You will feel yourself slow (figure 4.4).

There is no doubt you will probably fall quite a bit learning how to stop, but this is where all the pretraining and techniques for getting yourself back up come in. Your legs are sure to burn after practicing this for a while. It's like staying in a squat position for a very long time. You may experience some cramping. If so, sit down and stretch out your legs. If the pain is persistent, take a break off your board and shake out your legs.

To learn the second method, the uphill stopping technique, start by using the belly method to get into a standing position. With your entire body facing uphill and your board horizontal, push yourself off the ground and stand. Make sure you have plenty of room for this technique. As noted, you should always be aware of what's below you first and foremost, and this is difficult to do when you are facing uphill.

FIGURE 4.4   THE HEEL PRESS METHOD OF STOPPING.

FIGURE 4.5 THE UPHILL METHOD OF STOPPING.

To perform the stop, press the toe-side edge of your board into the snow, and lift your heels slightly. Staying bent and low as you place more pressure on your toe-side edge will bring you to a stop (figure 4.5). Think not about pointing and standing on the top of your toes, but instead about pushing your toes down as if you were standing on the balls of your feet. Many beginner riders make the mistake of taking the toe-side edge instruction too literally, which in turn makes them fall forward. Stay entirely facing uphill with your board horizontal in order to stop.

Turning

Once you get the hang of stopping in at least one direction, you should start learning how to turn. Turning, or carving as it is known, is the general movement you will be making while snowboarding. It will be how you control the board and what gets you down the hill. Learning how to link turns (both your heel and toe-side edges) is what usually takes beginners the longest to learn. Once you get the feeling of linking turns, it's just a matter of practice in order to perfect the motion and gain speed down the hill.

On the first day out, linking turns shouldn't really be a thought. You should concentrate on learning how to stop and getting at least your toe or heel-side down. That is a lot to achieve in one day, and you should be proud if you can do all that.

It will take some time before linking turns becomes natural. Just like figuring out which foot forward you are most comfortable with, you will find either the toe-side or heel-side turn is easier for you right away. Although learning heel-side is safer because you will be facing downhill, perfecting toe-side is generally easier because of the gravity of you facing uphill. It's usually easier for people to lean in a toe-side direction.

TOE-SIDE TURNS

Begin practicing toe-side turns by facing uphill in the stopped position. Your entire body and board should be facing uphill. Start to maneuver your body downhill, with your front foot leading. You will instantly feel yourself start to catch speed. To control yourself, turn your front foot back uphill, and stop yourself gently. Don't forget to keep your knees bent the *entire* time. If it feels as if you have no control, stop and visualize what you are supposed to be doing. Watch others who are riding down the mountain.

The best way to turn yourself back and forth is to think about starting from the head down. First you want to look in the direction you want to go. If you are riding regular (left foot forward), this is what you would do. Facing uphill and standing in a stopped position, turn your head left to look sideways downhill. Next turn your shoulders, hips, and feet in that direction so your left foot is pointed downhill and the back of your board is facing

A

B

uphill. Don't look down. Always look up and around you. Looking down will only make you fall. As you are gaining speed, you will want to turn your board back uphill to stop on your toe side. Look back up the hill, turning your shoulders, hips, and legs behind you. Press firmly down on the toe-side edge of your board as you are bringing your foot around to face uphill. You should essentially be doing a C motion back and forth.

If you ride goofy (right foot forward), you will be doing the exact same movement looking toward the right side of the hill instead of the left. Think of pressing into the snow and into your turn on the toe-side edge of your board. Let up on your toes as you are turning your board sideways, almost so you are not on the edge at all. You want to have a pretty flat foot when you are riding down sideways, but remember the less edge you are on, the faster you will start to go. Stay in control as much as possible at first by letting off gently as you turn sideways and then pressing firmly on your toe side when you are turning back uphill. Keep practicing, and you will soon perfect your toe edge and your stopping while facing uphill.

C

D

HEEL-SIDE TURNS

To learn heel-side turns you simply go in an opposite C. Begin practicing from the heel-side stop position with your entire body and board facing downhill. The same rules apply except you will be pressing on the heel side of your board instead of your toes. Remember to ride with bent knees, stay loose, and always look up and around you. Something that makes it easier for beginners to learn both toe and heel-side turns is pointing your finger in the direction you want to go. This essentially makes you turn one way or another. After you perfect both edges, you will ride with your arms loose by your sides.

A

B

To begin the turn from the heel-side stop position, let up and flatten yourself out as you face sideways down the hill again. Your front foot should always be pointed downhill when you are beginning. As you get better, you should start practicing riding switch (opposite of what you usually ride). Until then, stay with your leading foot always pointing downhill when you are riding. From head to toe, again turn your head to the side of the heel, followed by your shoulders, hips, and legs. You want to maintain a grip on your heel edge, but don't overcompensate. Now turn back downhill with your front foot leading, and continue to practice heel-side turning and stopping.

C

D

LINKING TURNS

When you learn how to link turns, that's when you are officially snowboarding. Linking turns, or carving, is the linking of both the toe- and heel-side edges over and over again. You will notice snowboarders ride in an S pattern. This is what you are shooting for. You want to ride sideways down the hill, back and forth, forming an S shape.

A   B   C

Begin on whichever edge is easier for you. If you are partial to the toe side, for example, start and turn as described in the section Toe-Side Turns. But instead of turning back uphill to stop, continue turning your board and your body downhill so that you stop on your heel-side edge. You have just linked turns! You want to continue turning uphill and then downhill, over and over again. Toe side, then heel side, toe side, then heel side. Keep looking up, and if it helps, use your finger to point in the direction you want to go. And, as always, keep your knees bent at all times.

D

E

F

TAKING LESSONS

Taking lessons from an instructor is highly recommended, especially when you are just starting out. Having someone quickly pinpoint what you are doing wrong and show you what to do right is very important and will only help you become a better snowboarder faster. Private lessons are the most hands on. It doesn't have to be just one on one; you can take private lessons with a few friends or siblings if you prefer. Lessons are generally an hour long, and the goal for the first session is to get you up the chairlift and down the hill once. You will likely not be linking turns your first time or even your 10th time down the hill, but linking turns is the eventual goal.

Group lessons are also beneficial if you like doing activities in a group or don't have the money to spend on private lessons. Resorts usually offer beginner packages that feature equipment rental, a lesson, and a lift ticket for a set price. You can prebook lessons before you arrive, but usually there are enough instructors on hand to get you in that same day. A group lesson is also about an hour in length, with the same goal as a private lesson. The only drawback with group lessons is they can sometimes be crowded with people of all ages, and it might be difficult to fully grasp the concept.

The bottom line is that any lesson with a reputable instructor is better than no lesson. It's not a bad idea to take a few beginner lessons and then move up in levels in order to grasp linking turns. The sooner you get the basic moves down, the sooner you'll be ready for action.

Progressing

Progression comes from dedicating yourself to the sport and taking the time to practice. If you think you can't do something in the first place, then you've already set yourself up for failure. If you have an open mind and a positive attitude and are willing to put yourself out there, you will not only get better at snowboarding but also grow as a person. Sometimes riders progress quickly; sometimes it takes years. If you have the right mind-set and a good group of friends who encourage you to try new maneuvers and go faster, then you are sure to succeed. Just don't put pressure on yourself. You are there to have *fun*!

Be in Control, Stay in Control

Establishing and maintaining control may seem like the hardest thing to do when you first start snowboarding. Even after taking some beginner lessons, watching videos, and reading up on the sport, you may still have moments when you struggle to get your board to do what you want it to and take you where you want to go. Remind yourself that you control your board; it doesn't control you. Be confident and assertive. Have faith in yourself, and be brave.

You have to be smart, especially when you're a beginner. Don't overstep your boundaries. Know your limits, and know where you are comfortable riding. Be confident and positive, but check yourself. Don't put yourself and others in dangerous situations. The last thing you want to do is injure yourself or someone else. If someone is trying to push you to ride somewhere you would not be comfortable, don't feel bad about saying no. Veteran riders are not impressed by beginners who think it's funny to try to do more than they can handle or who head straight for the roughest slopes to try to prove how tough they are. You aren't better than anyone else, and you don't have the right to put others at risk. Be respectful of others—even skiers. Seriously, be safe and be smart.

Although wearing appropriate safety gear is certainly important, it's just as important to know the riders' code and the rules you must follow on the mountain. If you ignore the rules and decide you are so cool you can do whatever you want to, you may actually get kicked off the mountain or even get blacklisted. Some snowboarding venues have begun adopting stricter guidelines, requiring riders to pass a written and riding test before they can shred certain areas of the resort and parks. The rules are for your own good.

Every venue has signs posted around the mountain. Watch for and read the signs, and follow the directions. If an area is closed, it's closed for a reason.

The number one rule at resorts worldwide is *be in control, stay in control*.

Rating System

The rating system at resorts makes it simple to measure your ability and understand which runs are more difficult than others. Getting to know the color and shape combos will literally lead you in the right direction. One thing worth mentioning is every resort uses similar color and shape combos to differentiate the levels of its runs; however, each resort rates according to its own mountain.

A color and shape combo basically symbolizes the range of the slope. Green circles signify the easiest, flattest runs, while double black diamonds represent the steepest, most difficult of runs. Work your way up, not vice versa. A potentially amazing day can turn south quickly if you go somewhere you shouldn't be going in the first place. If you're not familiar with the mountain, pick up a trail map before you go anywhere. Study it and know which runs suit your riding best, first and foremost. Here's a rundown of what you need to know about terrain labeling and resort signage to make your riding experience the best possible.

On Piste

This is the general rating system for all North American resorts. Remember that the ratings indicate how the slopes at that venue compare with one another—a slope rated "easy" in one location may be harder or easier than one with the same rating at another resort.

Green Circles

A green circle symbolizes the easiest of runs. These are generally the flattest and most manageable for beginner riders. Green slopes are often wider than most and always groomed. Start here if you are a beginner or are new to the resort.

Blue Squares

The blue square means the run is easy to intermediate. These are somewhat steeper and possibly narrower runs. Intermediate terrain is designated for riders who are confident linking turns, gaining speed, and stopping but who are not ready to hit really steep runs. If you're feeling stable and confident on the easy runs, test your skills on the blue square slopes. Remember to still look for runs with lots of space, and always know how to get back to the base in case you are having trouble. If you feel out of control or are feeling helpless, *take your time*. You should always ride with a buddy, preferably one who rides about the same level, but remember to have fun first and foremost. Take a breather on the side of the run visible to uphill riders, refocus, and try again.

Black Diamonds

Black diamonds symbolize intermediate to more advanced terrain. The slopes are steeper and more difficult, and they may or may not be groomed. Bring your A game and stay alert. Always work your way up to black diamonds and be aware of their locations. If you end up on a black and you are struggling, try to find a more mellow way down or ask where an easier run is.

Double Black Diamonds

Not all mountains rank double blacks, but if they do you should be aware of them. Double blacks are the most difficult runs for advanced to expert riders only. They are narrow, ungroomed, steep runs that are extremely hard to ride down unless you are very experienced and skilled. It may take years before you can ride double blacks, but it should be something you strive for. They are the most challenging and really test your capabilities as a snowboarder.

Freestyle Terrain

Orange ovals represent freestyle terrain. This usually means there are hand-built freestyle features to watch for, including but not limited to jumps, rails, boxes, wall rides, and halfpipes. The trail will be labeled separately, but the orange oval means that freestyle "extreme" obstacles exist. Mountains have started designating zones for freestyle features so that riders know what they can expect. Remember to continually look out for signage when you're in the freestyle or park sector.

Small Ovals

Signs labeled small mean the most minimal freestyle features, including ride-on boxes and jibs and the smallest of jumps. Although the small sign may vary slightly between resorts, it's a good starting place for beginner park riders to gauge their ability. It's important to know what you can do on small features and feel confident before moving on to medium.

Medium Ovals

Medium features are jibs and jumps attempted by the majority of park riders. Make sure you are 100 percent dialed on the smalls before you hit mediums. Medium features are generally on a little steeper slope and will feature ollie-on jibs. Jumps are higher consequence, yet not competition level or high risk. They are good training jumps. When you have nailed the medium features, you can think about attempting the bigger ones.

Large Ovals

Large signs symbolize the most challenging, highest-consequence features. Do *not* attempt large features unless you have dialed in the mediums. Large features take a higher skill set, with more confidence and knowledge of speed control and body awareness. Large-feature runs are often on steeper grades, and most riders find them scary just to look at. These are the toughest features in the park. Attempting and landing large features may be thrilling, but they can be dangerous if you don't have the proper training and practice.

The Responsibility Code

You are taking on a responsibility to yourself and to others when you hit the mountain. It is mandatory that snowboarders of all levels and all types abide by the Responsibility Code developed by the National Ski Areas Association (NSAA) and implemented by resorts worldwide. The waiver on the back of your ticket and the agreement you sign for your season pass include these regulations and say that you agree to abide by them. The NSAA and the resort owners didn't make up a bunch of ridiculous rules just to annoy you; they established the code to create a safe environment for everyone on the hill. The whole point is to prevent injuries and save lives. Take the rules and your responsibility to follow them seriously. You are there to have fun, of course, but following these simple rules won't spoil your fun; it will help ensure that everyone has a safe and enjoyable time. You can't prevent another person from riding out of control, but you can keep these guidelines in mind every time you step on the hill, which encourages others to do the same.

The seven rules of the Responsibility Code presented here are from National Ski Patrol's website (www.nsp.org/slopesafety/respcode.aspx). After each rule is some information from us on how to apply it.

1. **Always stay in control, and be able to stop or avoid other people or objects.** If you are having control problems, head for the area with fewest people. Do yourself and everyone else a favor and be smart. Practice, practice, practice until you know how to handle your board and yourself safely.

2. **People ahead of you have the right of way. It is your responsibility to avoid them.** As with driving a car, you must always be aware of what's in front

of you. It's good to know what's behind you as well, but because we don't have eyes in the back of our heads, you aren't expected to. If you crash into someone in front of you, you can be held responsible for injuries or damage. Again as when driving, where you look is where you'll go. If you see someone in front of you and think you are beginning to get out of control, look in the direction of an open area and try to stop as quickly as possible. You don't want to slam to the ground to avoid running into someone else and end up injuring yourself. Do what you can to stop safely.

3. **You must not stop where you obstruct a trail or are not visible from above.** Always try to stop on the side of a trail. Do *not* hang around on the ground in the middle. If you fall and need to take a break before you can continue, slide to the side and out of the way of others. If you are on a steeper hill, move to an area where you can see a good distance above you. You can't control the speed and skill of other riders, so don't put yourself in a situation where you are not visible. If you can't see them, they can't see you. Just because you have the right of way in this scenario doesn't mean you should stop wherever you choose and expect others to move around you.

4. **Whenever starting downhill or merging into a trail, look uphill and yield to others.** This is another rule that is similar to a driving rule. Look both ways before entering or merging into an area where others are riding. Most mountains have merging trails, especially toward the base area. Watch for signs indicating merging trails, and look uphill to cross traffic before proceeding. It's sometimes hard to gauge where other riders are headed, especially if they are swerving or carving back and forth. Wait for others who look as if they don't know where they're going to pass, then proceed. When you are passing someone, allow plenty of space and call out "On your right" or "On your left" as an added safety precaution.

5. **Always use devices to help prevent runaway equipment.** Leashes used to be mandatory for snowboarders. You used to have to wear a ropelike thing hooked on your front binding that you snapped onto your boot. As a safety precaution, these are often recommended for beginners. Although it's almost impossible to lose control of your board while you are strapped to it, when you're first strapping in and out a lot, you could send your board flying down the hill by itself if you're not careful. If your board is unstrapped completely for whatever reason, always make sure it is flipped bindings down and sideways to the slope, and not pointed downhill. If you simply set it down on the base, it may slide right down the hill and cause injury or ruin your equipment.

6. **Observe all posted signs and warnings. Keep off closed trails and out of closed areas.** This is self-explanatory. If you don't care to read and abide by the rules, then you shouldn't be on the mountain. Don't ever question posted warnings. Unless you want to get your ticket taken away and possibly get fined, follow the posted signs and you will be good to go.

7. **Prior to using any lift, you must have the knowledge and ability to load, ride, and unload safely.** Take a beginner lesson, and do whatever you need to be sure you can load and unload without incident. Read posted signs on loading instructions at the bottom of the lifts. If after doing all that you are

still unsure you can handle the process on your own, ask a lift attendant to help you. Once at the top, get off the lift and move out of the way of riders on the next chair.

You will notice signs around the mountain stating, "Know the Code. It's Your Responsibility." These postings serve as a reminder. Study the rules, and be safe out there.

Smart Style

Smart Style is a terrain park safety initiative the National Ski Areas Association and Burton designed for riders entering freestyle territory. Most of the rules stated are based on common sense, but whether you're new to park riding or you've been hitting the jibs for some time, take a minute to review the precautions you should take when you enter the park zone.

When you hit the park, don't just aim for having a cool style, aim for having Smart Style, too. Taking on the park can be scary and intimidating as a newbie. Making sure you know the proper etiquette and how not to annoy other people is important when it comes to park riding. Again, know your boundaries. Try tricks on the smaller features first. Proceed to the bigger features once you have a solid grasp of the concept of riding boxes and rails and hitting jumps. Progression is what it's all about, but don't go too big too soon. Follow the Smart Style rules and you're sure to become a better all-around rider and make friends at the park.

The Smart Style initiative has four main points. Remember and follow these rules when entering the park zone.

1. **Make a plan.**
   ◦ Every time you use freestyle terrain, make a plan for each feature you want to use.
   ◦ Your speed, approach, and takeoff will directly affect your maneuver and landing.

2. **Look before you leap.**
   ◦ Before getting into freestyle terrain, observe all signage and warnings.
   ◦ Scope around the jumps first, not over them.
   ◦ Use your first run as a warm-up run to familiarize yourself with the terrain.
   ◦ Be aware that the features change constantly because of weather, usage, grooming, and time of day.
   ◦ Do not jump blindly, and use a spotter when necessary.

3. **Easy style it.**
   ◦ Know your limits, and ski or ride within your ability level.
   ◦ Look for small-progression parks or features to begin with, and work your way up.
   ◦ Freestyle skills require maintaining control on the ground and in the air.
   ◦ Do not attempt any features unless you have sufficient ability and experience to do so safely.
   ◦ Inverted aerials increase your risk of injury and are not recommended.

4. **Respect gets respect.**
- ○ Respect the terrain and others.
- ○ One person on a feature at a time.
- ○ Wait your turn and call your start.
- ○ Always clear the landing area quickly.
- ○ Respect all signs, and stay off closed terrain and features.

Forming an X above the head lets the rider above know that it isn't safe to proceed.

ATML Method

Snowboarders use the ATML (approach, takeoff, maneuver, and landing) method to handle features and confidently land tricks in a safe way.* Each feature can be broken down into four zones. Identify these zones and plan your run before using any feature.

Approach zone is the space for setting your speed and stance to use the feature.

Takeoff zone is for making moves that start your trick.

Maneuver zone is for controlling your body in the air and setting up for landing.

Landing zone is the prepared slope between the knuckle and the runout beyond it.

The approach zone is also called the run-in zone. It's where a rider gains speed and prepares for the feature. Other riders should stay out of this zone. Although these areas aren't always marked, there is generally a small ridge or area a ways out where riders prepare to hit the feature. For bigger features, riders who are waiting to drop in often stand a good distance above the feature. Depending on the type and size of the

*ATML is a registered trademark of the American Snowsports Education Association (ASEA). Reprinted from www.terrainparksafety.org with permission from National Ski Areas Association.

feature, the drop-in zone may be larger or smaller. Watch where others are starting and proceed safely when able.

The takeoff zone is the prespin or preattempt zone just before you hit the feature as you begin to start the trick. This is the area close to the lip, or the buildup of snow next to the feature. You will begin to ollie, or jump, and prepare yourself here to get onto the jib or up in the air if you're doing a jump. The lip of a feature may be described as poppy if it easily sends you in the air, and a jib if it flings you onto it. This can be good or bad depending on what type of trick you are trying and how much board control you have because it means that you can perform bigger or more technical tricks, but it may be harder to stay in control.

The maneuver zone is the area between the takeoff and landing of the trick. It's the fun zone! Whether you're attempting the most basic of tricks, a straight air on a jump, or 50-50 on a rail, the maneuver zone is where you must execute the main part of the trick. It's important to stay in control and stay confident because this is where your skills are tested. While in the maneuver zone, you spot your landing and begin to prepare to land.

The landing zone is the reward zone immediately following the maneuver zone. This is where you stay focused through the end of the feature and finish in style as you bring the board down onto the snow and head for level terrain again.

The rules of Smart Style and the ATML method are exceptional guidelines to follow when you progress to the park. Study them, understand them, and then get out there and show off your skills.

Ride Any Terrain

Sure, now you are getting the hang of snowboarding, but where do you go from here? How do you push yourself to the next level?

As you work your way from the easier to the harder slopes, remember that although resorts use the same rating system, the ratings are relative to each resort. Just because you were riding intermediate slopes at one resort doesn't mean you should be going straight for them at another. The difficulty of a black diamond path (a steep, advanced run) may vary greatly from one resort to the next. The basic rules apply, but learn about the type of mountain and terrain you can expect to be riding by familiarizing yourself with a trail map. Study the areas that fit your riding ability. If you're new to the mountain and still getting the feel of making turns, try out the beginner slopes first and see how you feel. Easing your way toward the more difficult slopes is a far safer and more enjoyable approach than suddenly finding yourself in a situation that is beyond your skill set.

Freestyle Fun

Freestyle riding consists of taking on hand-built features such as jumps and rails as well as natural terrain features such as cliffs, rocks, gullies, and poppers. Although the park is labeled as freestyle terrain, any terrain on the mountain, even the most basic of runs, can provide freestyle opportunities. Natural features are fun to try, but they are usually not kept up, whereas the park is maintained by a park staff who regularly manicure the lips, landings, and all parts of the features. Ride natural terrain at your own risk—don't hit anything when you can't see the landing or don't know what's on the other side. Stay smart.

When hitting up freestyle terrain in the park, start in the small park and gradually work your way to the intermediate. Wear a helmet. And of course have fun! Practice makes perfect. Take it slow and be cautious, but don't think *too* much because that can actually work against you. Don't get so caught up in thinking about every little logistic that you fail to trust yourself and simply go with the flow. You're going to make mistakes, and you're going to fall. Deal with it. Just don't let it discourage you. You are a snowboarder now.

It's easy to get intimidated while riding park, especially when it's packed with riders who are being followed by filmers and look as if they're pros. Don't let it get to you. Just do your own thing, know your boundaries, and don't try to impress people. Although obviously you want to look as if you know what you're doing, you don't want to attempt something you aren't ready for just to try to look cool. Remember it's not a contest. Use the opportunity to watch more advanced riders to better your own style and skill.

Always be aware of everyone around you, and know your limits. Use the code. Wait your turn and be sure to let others know when you're dropping. Don't cut people off, and always wait until the rider in front of you is out of the landing before proceeding. Sometimes it may be difficult to see if it is clear to go. If this is the case, pass up the feature until the next run.

Riding in groups is always recommended. If you ride with a few people, often you will get to know their style and abilities. Feed off of the group dynamic and energy, and use it to watch out for and help each other. If you see someone fall on a feature and not get up, holler or signal to others not to proceed. Check if the person is okay, and call the ski patrol for help if the situation is serious. Blocking the feature with your board turned upside down, with the base facing up, will signal to others that it is not safe.

Freestyle snowboarding has exploded in popularity over the years, mainly since mountains are now expected to build a few jumps and jibs in order to bring riders to the mountain. No longer are most riders satisfied with riding down groomed trails. They want more. Although parks provide a more contained environment where riders can get more consistency on a day-to-day basis, freestyle riding on natural features can be equally as fun. Some people may not have any desire to enter the park, and that's completely fine. Not riding park doesn't mean you aren't going to advance and have fun. Do what you feel you are capable of.

Halfpipes and Quarterpipes

Learning to ride halfpipes and quarterpipes is like learning how to snowboard all over again. The entire feeling and momentum are quite different from just taking turns down the mountain. A halfpipe, if you aren't familiar with the term, is half a circle (think of a round pipe in the ground—clever, right?) carved by a specialized machine in order to create two walls (figure 6.1). Walls of the pipe are anywhere from a few feet on each side to 22 feet (6.7 m; the size of Olympic and X Games pipes) and around 85 degrees. A quarterpipe is half a halfpipe, of course—basically just one wall (figure 6.2).

Watching people ride the pipe, especially professionals, will give you a better idea of where your body should be and what you need to do. It's imperative to know how to ride in both directions (with your regular front foot forward and with the other foot forward) so you can land and ride away properly. Halfpipes at major resorts aren't really built for learning. They are generally too big for learners, with walls up to 22 feet—superpipe size. Practicing on a smaller quarterpipe or a mini-halfpipe is ideal.

Before dropping into a halfpipe, always be aware of the people around you—those in front and those behind you, waiting to go. Wait until the rider ahead of you has gone a quarter to halfway down the pipe if possible before proceeding. Once the area is clear, slide forward on your heel-side edge. (It's easier for riders to try on their heel side first.) If you are regular, try your regular foot forward first, taking a toe-side edge if you're hitting the right wall and a heel-side if you are trying the left wall. If you are goofy, it's the opposite.

FIGURE 6.1 HALFPIPE.

FIGURE 6.2 QUARTERPIPE.

Gain some speed until just before the start of the wall cut, then turn your body toward the opposite wall. Although you should remain on an edge to an extent, keeping your speed is very important when riding the pipe. Stay low with your knees bent as you approach the wall on your heel-side edge. As you approach the top of the wall, use all your momentum to pop, or ollie, up and turn your body in a frontside air (180 degrees) to face the opposite wall. Stay low and hold on to your momentum on your toe-side edge toward the opposite wall. As you reach the top, ollie off of your toes, and turn your body in a frontside air again to ride toward your heel-side wall. Repeat. This is a very basic way to ride a halfpipe, and whether it sounds easy or does not make sense, if you practice and watch others, you'll eventually get it. Just like first starting to snowboard, you will get one wall more easily than the other. Your goal is to get out of the pipe, catch air, frontside spin from both sides of the wall, and link them together. This might take years. Don't get discouraged. Halfpipe riding is an acquired skill, and it takes a ton of time and practice to master it. Once you get the hang of it and are able to get out of the pipe, you will feel as if you can take on the world. It is an awesome accomplishment.

Rails and Boxes

Rails and boxes are intimidating for almost anyone who just began snowboarding. Thinking about riding a board across a metal or plastic piece of hand-built material may not be appealing at all. But then again, if you're reading this then you must be somewhat interested. The truth is rails and boxes can be a fun experience and a cool way to develop your skill set on a snowboard. Of course they are challenging, but if you learn what to do when approaching, riding, and landing them, then you just might find yourself to be a jib master in no time.

Rails and boxes come in a variety of shapes and sizes. This can be one of the most intimidating factors of all. Lucky for you, most resorts have beginner boxes and rails.

Try flat boxes, preferably only a few feet long at first. These are the easiest features to learn on. Rails are usually more difficult because they are round. However, there are flat rails now, too.

The beginner area in a park should be apparent, but if it isn't, ask a worker at the mountain or look on the trail map. Parks that are sponsored by Burton designate single runs for beginners and riders looking to improve their skills in zones called Progression Parks. Look for these too when possible.

Once you find the zone, really hone in on what others are doing and take notes. You will notice right away what not to do. Remember the rules of riding park features from chapter 5. Make sure there is plenty of room and there are no other riders around the area before attempting the box.

You will need some speed when hitting features. Find a nice flat box that is almost completely set down in the snow. Start on a box you don't have to ollie, or jump up, onto. You want a smooth ride-on box first.

One of the biggest mistakes riders make is going too slowly. Watch others if possible to gauge the right speed for hitting a feature. Drop where everyone else does, and understand the speed to hit the box.

As you attempt to drop, make sure you're strapped in tightly. Face downhill on your heel-side edge with your feet horizontal. Turn your body as you normally would to ride down a run, with your front foot forward. You basically want to head directly toward

After you've mastered the beginner flat boxes, check out the wide variety of rail features, including the *(a)* flat box, *(b)* rainbow rail, and *(c)* flat rail.

the box. Try not to make any turns. Just keep a consistent edge and hold your speed. The number one rule in landing is to keep your eyes on the end of the feature and never ever look down. Just as when learning how to snowboard, always look in the direction you want to go when hitting a feature. Keep your knees bent, and as you approach the box, think about staying completely flat on your board, not pressing on an edge whatsoever. Pressing an edge equals destruction. You will crash if you press an edge, so think of pressing directly down in the center of your board and staying flat.

As you approach the box, keep your body sideways down the hill. Don't make any sudden turns or maneuvers. That comes later. Stay straight, with your nose in front and tail in back. With all of these things in place—keeping your speed, staying flat, and looking at the end of the feature—you should easily ride right onto the box. As your tail makes its way off the box, ride away, turn, and stop. You did it!

If you fall, it shouldn't be too serious off of this size and type of feature. Remember what you learned about how to fall properly, and use those tools to do so if it happens. If you get scared during your approach and decide not to follow through, try to make a quick turn away from the feature. Try not to crash and burn onto the feature. If you feel yourself falling off the feature, try to stay flat, keep your balance, and look to the end. If you fall, try not to fall onto the feature. Point your board off the side of the feature and move out of the way (in case someone is dropping next) as soon as possible.

As you keep practicing and are feeling confident riding boxes, try your skills on longer flat boxes and move up to rails. The same rules apply when riding rails. The feeling will be a little different, mainly because your entire board won't be on the rail and it takes a little more balance, but you should have a better idea what to do once you've got the hang of boxes.

After getting used to confidently riding straight (boardsliding) on boxes and rails, you will be able to start trying tricks and really showing people up.

Jumps

Jumps are the closest thing we as snowboarders have to flying. Being in the air and feeling the breeze is so freeing. If you're thinking about trying jumps, just like learning how to ride rails and boxes, look for small jumps in areas designated for beginners (figure 6.3). Again, watch others hit the jump first and gauge their speed. Wait your turn and then proceed with confidence. Finding the right speed on jumps is crucial.

FIGURE 6.3 THE SMALL JUMP IN A TERRAIN PARK IS A PERFECT PLACE TO LEARN TO HANDLE JUMPS AND BEGIN TO PRACTICE TRICKS.

Once you start riding bigger jumps (figure 6.4), controlling your speed and knowing the snow conditions from one day to the next become a mathematical equation.

You may see riders test their speed by riding up to a jump and then stopping on their heel side at the lip (very edge) of the jump. This is a good way to determine how fast or slow you need to go. However, if you're on a very small jump for your first time you won't need to do much speed checking. Just don't race as fast as you can toward the jump, and you should be okay.

When approaching a jump, gain your speed by staying straight; check your speed by turning a few times if necessary. As you come up to the lip, stay flat with your knees bent and pop, or ollie, off of the heel edge of your board. On jumps, always stay centered back on your board—don't lean forward. You need to pop off of a jump in order to really land properly. But if you get too much air and aren't expecting it, it can be scary. Try to stay calm if this occurs, and don't do anything drastic with your body. As you peak in the air and begin your descent, stay sideways downhill and land flat, with your back foot first. You will normally easily land and ride away if you stay flat and utilize that back foot. Ride away off of the landing and away from the jump, turning and stopping. You just landed a jump!

FIGURE 6.4 ONCE YOU HAVE YOUR JUMPING SKILLS DOWN, YOU CAN TAKE ON LARGER JUMPS, LIKE THIS SET IN THE TERRAIN PARK AT HEAVENLY RESORT IN LAKE TAHOE, CALIFORNIA.

Jumping takes a little time to get used to, but with lots of practice you should be able to quickly move to bigger jumps. Once you get the hang of it and are really feeling confident, you can begin trying to spin and do tricks off of jumps.

Other Features

You may notice a number of other natural or constructed features in the park. These include wall rides, picnic tables, bonks, rainbow boxes or rails, and C or S boxes or rails, to name a few. There are also many types of jumps including tabletops, hips, spines, and gaps. All these features require practice and skill to attempt. Stick to the basics first, and always work your way up from there.

Powder Rush

There is not another feeling in the world comparable to riding powder. Once you get the hang of it, the sense of freedom will make you dream of the next time you can do it again. There's a reason people live for first chair at a resort when it's snowed feet overnight, or hike hours just for one untouched line. Learning to ride powder, however, is a whole different story. The basics you've been taught about snowboarding really don't apply. Figuring out how to maneuver in bottomless snow and enjoy it takes added dedication and drive.

There is a technique to riding powder that is different from anything you have done on groomed resort runs. Getting comfortable riding in deep snow, staying afloat, and staying in control may, at times, feel like learning how to snowboard all over again. The main thing to remember when attempting to ride in fresh snow is to lean back. You must not only keep your knees and center of gravity low when attempting to shred powder but also position your body toward the tail of your board in order to stay on top of the snow and not sink. There will be times that your legs are burning, even if you've been riding powder for years, simply because of the weight and pressure you're putting on your thighs.

Positioning your bindings all the way back on your board will help remind you to lean back and help you get through deep snow. It's also not a bad idea to shorten your stance a little and turn both angles toward the nose of your board, unless you are planning on riding switch. Setting up your board in this manner gives you better board control and leverage through deep snow. You don't have to set up your board like Alpine skis, with your feet completely faced forward, but it's a good idea to at least try a few variations to see what's easier riding in this type of snow. A shorter stance will give you more board in the snow, and having more board touching the snow will help you get through it. A longer board and one made specifically for powder (narrower and stiffer) is also advised. A longer board will help you get more speed through the deep snow. You are trying to prevent sinking and getting stuck, which is sure to happen if you aren't used to riding in

For riders who've mastered the technique, feeling the rush in the back country is the ultimate snowboarding experience.

deep snow. Setting up your equipment to match the depth of the powder and type of snow (light or heavy) will really help your cause. Usually riders set their stance back and bring their feet a little closer together when riding in deeper snow in order to maintain better control.

You are sure to get frustrated while learning to ride in deep snow. When you fall, it is not a matter of simply getting right back up. If you fall in super deep snow, you might not be able to get out without taking your board off and patting down the snow. Although it may seem that "Try not to fall" is good advice, you'll have better success if you just go for it than if you try to be cautious and take it super slow. Powder isn't going to hurt when you fall into it, and that's the best part. Staying back on your tail with your knees bent will get you the feeling and ability to get through it. If you think you're going too fast, just stay calm and press on your toe- or heel-side edge in order to slow down. If you turn all the way to stop as you normally would on a groomer, you may find yourself bogged down by the snow, and this may cause you to fall.

Learning to ride powder can be scary because it's easy to go fast, but the more you ride it the better you will get at making powder turns and being able to stop and go smoothly. Plus, think about it: You aren't likely to fall and hurt yourself too seriously if you land in soft snow. Always have an exit strategy for when you're going too fast, and try to hold it together. Think positive, and use your balancing skills to regain control.

Make sure you are alert and energized before taking on riding powder. Getting stuck a few times will wear you out pretty quickly. If you are tired from the start, you'll be in for a frustrating and potentially short day.

Once you have your basic navigation skills dialed, getting down the hill and perfecting the slash is your ultimate goal. Concentrate on leaning back and putting a lot of pressure on the heel-side edge of your board. You may have heard that the feeling is like surfing, and this is close to true. It is a similar motion and feeling. When you are just starting out, keep facing downhill and don't make huge turns. Turning uphill as you usually would on a toe-side turn is likely to make you fall in the powder. To turn in powder, press slightly on the toe- or heel-side edge of your board, and avoid making big, wide turns. The best strategy is to keep your speed. Losing your speed can make you fall, so being able to go fast, especially on flatter spots in powder, will serve you well.

Practice on an open run at a resort, not on a groomer but close to one that is easily accessible so you can make your way in that direction if riding becomes too intense or tiring. Riding on a steeper slope will also help, preferably one that's wide open, where the snow is not too deep. A few feet of fresh snow is enough to get a feel for riding powder, and if you get stuck you'll be able to get yourself back up relatively easily.

As with linking turns, an understanding of how to ride powder will just suddenly come to you at some point. The first several times you attempt to ride in deep snow, you may feel like a complete rookie, even if you've been snowboarding for years. When everything clicks, though, it will be life changing. Some riders never look back and start refusing to ride resorts, instead going off in search of bottomless snow. This could happen to you one day. Be careful what you wish for!

Beyond the Boundaries

After you have several years of shredding experience under your belt, you may be tempted to try riding out of bounds. Carving untouched lines and exploring the mountains is an incredibly exciting and liberating experience. Many advanced riders thrive on the challenge and thrill of going out of bounds. Feeling free, unrestrained, and in the unknown is thrilling, but it can also be deadly. Beginners should absolutely not attempt it, and even veteran riders should give it careful consideration. The risk factors associated with backcountry snowboarding are appropriate for those of an expert or professional riding level only.

No resort recommends ducking ropes. The trails are marked and roped off for a reason. Understand the rules of the resort you are at, and proceed with caution. If you are caught riding out of bounds at a resort, you will usually get kicked off the mountain and fined as well. But there are far greater repercussions to venturing beyond the ropes.

There is no ski patrol, and there are no groomed runs or signs. Once you go out of bounds, you are on your own. You never know what you may find. That sweet line below might drop right off a cliff. The terrain can be deadly, and you should be confident that you know what to do in a life or death situation before you decide to risk it because you just might find yourself in such a situation. You have little to no chance of being rescued.

Preparation

You are literally putting your life on the line if you don't have the proper education and equipment to take out there. If you are thinking of heading out of bounds, take a few backcountry safety courses to start. Resorts may not have backcountry courses available because of liability issues, but check around town and through backcountry gear stores. Big mountain resorts that include rideable out-of-bounds terrain, set off by clear boundary lines, usually host clinics throughout the season to ensure that riders are aware of safety precautions and know what to do in difficult situations. Although each mountain is different, all mountains with off-piste accessibility should include clearly marked boundaries and caution signs notifying riders they are entering a possibly unsafe zone that is not managed by the resort. Always be aware and focused so that you don't end up somewhere you don't want to be.

On-mountain terrain is managed by the ski patrol and marked by the resort if it contains hazards such as cliffs and rocks, while backcountry terrain isn't marked at all. Avalanche bombs or dynamite is also set off on the mountain to prevent avalanches at the resort. These bombs help break up the snow if it is unstable to make the terrain safe. Although there is always a chance of an avalanche on runs at resorts, it is minimal in comparison to the chance of one occurring out of bounds. If you don't know about snowpack and what types of layers of snow you are riding on top of, you should not venture out of bounds. Make sure you understand the implications of riding on unmanaged areas and the type of terrain, including gullies and crevices that are prone to danger, before you even think of stepping out of bounds. Know before you go, and understand what you are getting yourself into before it is too late.

If you are riding out of bounds in an area where it snows a lot, you are putting yourself in avalanche territory. With no available ski patrol, it will be on you to dig yourself or your buddy out. With that possibility hanging over your head, taking an avalanche safety course is also encouraged. Check for local listings online and at www.avalanche.org for classes in your area. See the Avalanche Safety Tips section later in this chapter.

Proper safety equipment for the backcountry is highly recommended if not mandated, including a probe, shovel, and beacon. These items are precautionary in case an avalanche occurs and someone needs to be rescued. A beacon is a tracking device about the size of a walkie talkie; when turned on, it sends a signal to other similar devices announcing its location. This is what you need in order to find someone who has been buried and what you need to wear at all times (and have turned on) so others can find you. The beacon is worn at the waist, usually with a strap that goes across the shoulder and around the abdomen (under the jacket). Make sure your group is on the same frequency so you can easily track someone if a problem arises. The beacon is battery operated, so carry fresh batteries or make sure the loaded batteries have a lot of life left before venturing out. Turn the beacon on right before you head out of bounds. If you have to search for someone, simply change the setting to search, and the device will point you in the right direction via lighted arrows.

A probe and shovel are used to search for someone once you have tracked him and pinpointed his general location. The probe is compact, but you can extend it to reach down in the snow and feel where the person is buried. Once you know where and how deep he is, it's time to start digging. Using what you have learned in avalanche safety classes and have practiced with friends, you should be able to work systematically and in a rapid manner to get the person out as soon as possible.

If you choose to ride out of bounds, always be *overly* prepared. Here are a few items you should take on your journey:

- Beacon
- Probe
- Shovel
- Backpack
- Water
- Snacks
- Extra gloves
- Whistle
- Mirror to use as a reflector
- Phone or walkie talkie

Knowing what to do when you're out of boundary zones and get caught in a bad scenario is an absolute requirement. Every year there are stories of riders' bodies being found out of bounds or never being found at all. Don't do this to your friends and family. Think beyond the epic untouched snow you could be riding. Think the situation through thoroughly. If you are confident you have obtained the proper knowledge, skills, and equipment for hitting the backcountry, and you have no reservations, then go for it!

Protocol

The rules for riding the backcountry are much different from the rules for riding resorts. The backcountry rule to live by is "Never go alone." It is a bad call no matter how experienced you are or where you are going. Always take at least one other rider in case something does go wrong. This is extremely important. It's wise to go with someone who has been to the area before or can lead you around. It's easy to get lost out of bounds. Your cell phone will *not* save you. Not only is the chance of having service slim,

AVALANCHE SAFETY TIPS

Avalanches in the backcountry are more often than not caused by people riding in unsafe territory. According to avalanche.org, "90 percent of avalanche victims die in slides triggered by themselves or a member of their group." This is because avalanches usually start when an impact makes the snow move. This is also why avalanches sometimes occur after a few people have already gone over the surface. The pressure put on the snow may cause a slab of it to break off or slide and form an avalanche. If you don't understand snowpack and how the layers of snow and weather affect the terrain you are riding, you probably shouldn't be out of bounds in the first place. There's a whole science to snowpack, and understanding it is crucial for riding in the backcountry. Classes will help explain the intricacies of snowpack and how to know what kind of terrain you are dealing with. Riders will learn how to assess the snowpack by digging and reading layers of snow. This will help you figure out how easily the snow will slide and get set off if you ride over it.

As you venture out, reading the snow throughout your journey is key. The terrain and conditions may vary from place to place because of where the sun has hit it or if more snow has fallen in specific zones. Avalanche classes teach what to do if someone is buried, sometimes even burying people so that others can search and dig for them as practice.

The chances of winding up in a major avalanche are slim, so don't let that turn you away. Just know what to do if one does strike so you will be ready to go into search and survival mode. Taking avalanche classes prepares you to think quickly and make fast moves and decisions.

If you do get caught in a slide situation, *don't panic.* If you feel the snow moving underneath you, jump upslope. Try to get above the break line before it really begins sliding. If the avalanche starts in front of you (the best scenario), stop riding immediately. Remain calm and allow the snow to cascade down the mountain.

If the avalanche starts behind you, keep riding, try and stay on your feet, and stay on top of the snow for as long as possible. This is why it's important to be an advanced rider. If you are still having trouble remaining in control and feeling solid on a board, then you shouldn't be in the backcountry in the first place. If the snow continues to slide, ride as far to the side of a slope as you can. This will hopefully get you out of the path of the avalanche's destruction.

If you still can't escape, hold onto a tree or something stable. This will help prevent you from being buried. Hold on tight and breathe. If there is nothing to hold onto or you are still being whisked away, swim, as if catching a wave, to stay near the surface and avoid being buried.

If the white wave is too strong and you are becoming buried, create an air pocket around your mouth with your arms or hands. Obviously, the longer you are able to breathe, the better. Try to move around once the snow settles, but conserve your air as much as possible. If you don't know which way is up, spit and see which direction it goes. Wiggle your body toward the surface. You may be closer to the top than you think, and you might be able to get a hand to the surface. If you are too stuck to maneuver or too far down to dig out, remain calm and conserve your air supply. Your beacon will send a signal to other riders, who can dig you out.

A class on avalanche safety should educate you on how to use your beacon, how to search for someone, and how to dig someone out. It's imperative to take an efficient, systematic approach in order to reach the buried person in time, and these classes teach ways to maximize the efforts of the people on hand to reach the appropriate depth and to clear the snow safely.

the likelihood of the person on the other end of the call getting to you in time if something does go wrong is extremely unlikely.

Don't just fly off on your own and bolt down the mountain. Know what is around you and especially in front of you at all times. You can never be too cautious. Even if you've been to the area before, snow conditions and weather change daily. A warm-up lap is always wise. Stay aware, alert, and in control. You must be able to respond quickly and make a fast turn if necessary to avoid a sudden danger and to stay upright if you hit a rock or stump underneath the snow.

The basics of backcountry etiquette are simple. There is definitely safety in numbers, but you must be aware of where everyone is at all times. Follow each other strategically, and don't venture off if you are unsure of your location. You should always have a designated guide, a highly qualified backcountry rider, who can lead the way. Generally the most experienced should be the guide. Guides should be qualified and certified through tests and classes; they should be trained to read the snowpack and to determine which lines are safe to take on the way down.

Follow the leader down, and ride one by one, one section at a time. Never just mob down the hill and assume it's safe. The guide should go down first, stop after a few turns, and call out that it's safe. The other riders should meet the guide and stop. The trip should be a series of stop and go unless you can clearly see the entire slope below. Even then, always designate a spotter who can tell how the snow is sliding underneath and where not to ride. If it's pretty wide open, have the guide head down first. Once you can see that the guide is safely at the bottom, you can cruise on down and enjoy the ride. Never veer too far away from your partners. You should always try to remain in sight.

Many riders like to hike up to higher off-piste ridges as well. Hiking itself can be insane work if you aren't prepared, haven't hiked a lot, and haven't trained for this type of exertion. Understand that it may take you some time to get to the top. Take it slow. Don't be in a major hurry. Just stay calm and enjoy the surroundings. The best advice is to follow bootpack, or a trail someone else has created, so you aren't continually sinking in the snow. If you must break trail yourself, take your time and conserve your energy. If you are climbing to a popular hiking spot, take advantage of the information other skiers and riders there can provide. Follow their lead, talk with them about which drop-ins are good, and find your own line. This is when snowboarding is truly about the adventure and experience. It's exhilarating and fulfilling to hike for your lines and ride where no one else has ridden.

There are sure to be plenty of trees and glades surrounding you in the backcountry. Trees are super fun and challenging, but they are also one of the main causes of injury on the slopes. Riding trees and glades takes tremendous skill in making quick turns and in focusing on and responding to what is in front of you. Even if you are used to making quick turns, having a big fat tree dead ahead can be daunting. Remember to look in the direction you want to go. Do *not* stare at the tree in your path; look past it and focus on your line around it. In areas with deep or heavy snow, trees can develop tree wells, open areas surrounding the tree where wind or the tree itself has prevented snow from building up normally. The snow in the well is loose and unconsolidated, and riders can quickly be trapped. Keep a wide distance from the trees.

Practice where the trees are well spread out. Use the areas on the resort right off to the side of most runs where the trees separate the slopes. You can quickly and easily get back on a groomed run if you are having difficulties. Move yourself in and out of the trees as you get the hang of riding through them and maneuvering around. After you have built up your skills and confidence, you can ride the trees out of bounds.

There are many skills involved in riding the backcountry. If you prepare well and take it seriously, your adventures in the quiet, wide-open spaces will be everything you hoped for.

Studying and practicing before you go can make the difference between life and death. Learn and practice CPR, too, in case the person who has been dug out isn't breathing.

With the right attitude, combined with some preparation and practice, you can ride any terrain that appeals to you!

Advanced Riding

Y ou've been through the basics, and you should now be ready to push your skills. In part III we'll introduce you to tricks and how to execute them. In chapter 7 we'll take you through the basic tricks in step-by-step fashion so you can perform them on your own. Photos and illustrations will help show you exactly what to do. We also offer advice on what *not* to do so you stay safe and continue having fun.

Take your riding farther in chapter 8 with more step-by-step instructions on advanced tricks as well as advice on getting past some common errors.

In chapter 9 we offer pointers on staying strong and healthy, and we toss in some snowboard-specific exercises to keep you on top of your game.

To cap it all off, in chapter 10 we'll let you in on what it's like to compete and even to venture into the professional world of snowboarding. We'll tell you about the various types of competitions and what it takes to win so you can decide if and at what level you want to compete. Good luck on your journey and keep the shred alive!

Introduction to Tricks

So you think you're ready to step it up and try some tricks? Well, let's go! There is no set time frame that indicates when you're ready to try tricks. It all depends on your own capabilities and skill, with a little motivation and validation thrown in. The important thing is to get the simpler component moves dialed in before you move on to the harder, more complicated tricks. Trying too soon to do a trick that involves multiple steps is beyond risky and could lead to an injury that keeps you off the slopes and sets back your progression.

Many resorts have programs and instructional freestyle coaches who can help you do anything and everything you have ever seen or can imagine. Finding groups through a local resort or school is a good start. You will have someone to guide you and others who are at the same level, trying to learn the same things. It's fun to have other people to share the process with, and it's a great way to meet friends and expand your social set.

The Burton Snowboard Academy at Northstar California Resort is a great option for those in the Tahoe region or who can travel there. The Burton Academy is designed for the intermediate to advanced rider looking to progress in the park sector. Riders receive hands-on instruction while dialing in their skills in a fun and friendly environment. There are many weekend programs, as well as groups and clubs that cater to people who don't live close to resorts.

Quite a few mountain towns have snowboard schools that are designed to really push and enhance potential professional-level riders. These schools provide academic instruction while encouraging snowboarding development. In a sense, snowboarding is a part of the curriculum.

Snowboard high schools and academies are the ultimate option for day-to-day training. At the establishments listed in table 7.1, aspiring pros can work toward a diploma or degree while getting high-caliber training on the slopes every day. Accredited coaches teach riders both on and off the hill to be the best snowboarder and scholar they can be.

If you are determined to learn tricks, whether or not you attend a school or academy, the most important piece of advice, as with learning to snowboard in general, is to watch, watch, watch. Watch videos, watch competitions, watch other riders on the hill. After you understand what you are supposed to be doing, begin to visualize yourself doing the trick. Most pros will tell you that visualization is their number one tool when it comes to learning new tricks. Seeing yourself complete the trick in your head from start to finish will ultimately help you pull off the trick and landing. Once you see and understand the trick, it's mind over matter. If you know it's possible and you believe you can do it, then you are destined to succeed.

TABLE 7.1 SNOWBOARD SCHOOLS AND ACADEMIES

Carrabassett Valley Academy 3197 Carrabassett Drive Carrabassett Valley, ME 04947	**Park City Snowboard Academy** PO Box 680719 Park City, UT 84068-719
Vail Ski and Snowboard Academy 1951 South Highway 24 Minturn, CO 81645	**Windells Academy** 59550 E Highway 26 Sandy, OR 97055
Mt. Mansfield Winter Academy PO Box 3269 Stowe, VT 05672	**Sun Valley Ski Academy** PO Box 2118 Sun Valley, ID 83353
Burton Snowboard Academy Northstar California Resort 5001 Northstar Drive Truckee, CA 96161	**Rossland Secondary School** 2390 Jubilee Street PO Box 1238 Rossland, BC V0G 1Y0
Squaw Valley Academy 235 Squaw Valley Road Olympic Valley, CA 96146	

Airs and Spins

Following are descriptions and instructions for the basic tricks that are the root of every other advanced trick in snowboarding: the ollie, the switch, and the 180.

Read the information, learn the steps, and then visualize and practice these tricks over and over again. You can use these tricks individually to keep things interesting or expand on them and become the ultimate trickster.

OLLIE

You have probably already ollied and not even known it. An ollie is basically using your momentum to jump up off the ground. The snowboard ollie is a derivative of the skateboarding maneuver in which the skater presses down on the back of the board and pops straight up in the air while keeping the board close to his feet. Learning an ollie takes some patience, but overall it just takes practice.

Learning to ollie, or pop, as it is often called, high off the ground and control your body will help you perform spins and a multitude of tricks. The best way to practice is to be strapped in on a mellow to flat area of snow if you aren't sure what to do. Add in the element of sliding down the hill after you feel comfortable doing ollies on flat ground. Combining the jumping with riding down the hill will come later.

Standing in your natural stance with your front foot facing downhill, your goal is to press on the nose of your board while leaning your weight a good amount forward. Think of your body and legs moving in an almost snakelike motion. Pressing and leaning on your nose, use your momentum to then shift all your weight to the tail of your board, springing off of your back foot. As you shift your weight to the tail of the board, you'll press hard and use your weight to lift first your front foot off the ground and then your back. The weight shift and momentum should automatically spring you up into the air, but you can visualize lifting up off the ground as well. The strength of the motion of your feet and the shift in body weight provide the height in the ollie.

You want to pop in the air, keeping your knees bent and staying in the same position as you would normally be riding down the mountain, with your front foot angled forward downhill. Allow your arms to move freely, using them to help you with balance if need be. When most riders ollie, their arms usually float out to the sides so they are making a T. Don't let thinking about your arms hinder your attempt at ollieing. Allow your arms to move naturally throughout the movement.

As you come down, you should always try to land on your back foot because landing on your front may cause your body to fling forward, making it more difficult to catch yourself and ride away. Land flat and lightly on your tail, then on your nose, centering yourself back up to try again. You don't want or need a dramatic one-two motion or a long pause between landing the tail and landing the nose; you just want to ease the tail

A   B   C

down first. This happens pretty naturally because you are typically ollieing on an angled hill. Keeping your knees well bent and staying low throughout the ollie will help you get higher in the air. Do *not* straighten your legs. While you are popping the ollie and while you're in the air, keeping your knees well bent is key, but feel free to land and ride away with your legs slightly bent and loose as you do normally riding down the hill.

Some types of snowboards make ollieing easier. Refer to the discussion of different decks for different riding styles in chapter 2. Generally the softer and poppier the board, the easier it will be to ollie. It doesn't mean you can't ollie with a stiffer, backcountry or big mountain deck. It just means it will take a little more energy and effort to ollie higher. Park-specific boards are softer to make it easier to nail tricks. But whatever you ride, if you invest some time and energy, learning to do a basic ollie will come pretty naturally. You aren't going to have to think hard about doing it or put a great deal of effort toward just getting up in the air. Working on tweaking it out or doing a grab is tougher—but that will come later.

Once you understand the concept and feel secure about your ollieing skills, it's time to take it to a run. It is easier to ollie on little bumps in the snow and small jumps too, since there is a little something there to help you pop into the air.

OLLIE INSTRUCTIONS

1. Get low and bend your knees.
2. Stay low and press forward, using momentum to slide your board forward.
3. Load the tail, pressing all your weight on the tail of your board (your nose should be lifted off the snow).
4. Pop in the air, keeping your knees more bent than usual. Think of bringing them out in front of you as if you are sitting in a chair floating in the air. As you come down, you should straighten your knees slightly as you return to your normal riding position.
5. Land with your back foot first, lightly and flat on the snow, followed by your front. Just think of keeping your weight a little more on the back foot and tail of the board, as opposed to the front. You will essentially land on both feet at almost the same time, with your back foot hitting the snow first, which provides some stability.
6. Ride away and try it again.

D   E   F

SWITCH

Being able to ride both regular and goofy is going to improve your snowboarding and help you learn new tricks. If you feel comfortable and are able to go fast riding switch, your options for learning and landing new tricks are limitless. Being a good switch rider also means you will be able to get out of sketchy situations more easily.

One of the main advantages of being able to ride switch is that you can land half spins. Typically the first spin a rider learns is the 180 (a half spin), and being able to land and ride away in the opposite direction makes the learning process much easier. Whether you learn to spin frontside, with your back shoulder coming in front of your body, or backside with your front shoulder turning in toward your back and uphill, your switch skills will come into play.

Riding switch means doing the exact same sequence of moves as when riding normally, as far as heel- and toe-side turns, but in the opposite direction and with the opposite foot. But if you've ever tried to write with your nondominant hand, you know that's not as easy as it sounds. At times learning to ride switch will make you feel like a beginner all over again. The good thing is you already know what to do; you just need to perfect doing it in the opposite direction.

Because you already understand the concepts involved and have a feel for snowboarding, motivation and practice are all it takes to dial in your switch. The hardest part is already over. You'll be applying, but modifying, the basic techniques from chapter 4. With continued practice you will be able to ride switch without thinking twice.

Take the time to really master riding switch. Dedicate several full days of riding to the task. Make yourself ride down entire runs switch. Get back on the starter slopes and be okay with it. Beginner slopes help you obtain better control and focus as a rider so you can get a trick down. It's easy to get hindered by faster riders or people performing more advanced tricks when practicing something new on intermediate or advanced terrain. Beginner terrain offers more wide-open space and gives you more opportunities to ride switch more confidently. Start gradually and work your way to more advanced runs.

Putting in the time to practice riding switch is for your own good. Solid switch riding expands your trick repertoire, which gives you more ways to have fun on the slopes. It also opens the door to becoming an advanced rider or possibly a professional snowboarder.

RIDING SWITCH INSTRUCTIONS

1. Start on a beginner hill, facing uphill on your toe-side edge on the opposite side of your board than you usually ride on.
2. Stay low and centered on your board, with your knees bent.
3. Look uphill (always keep your eyes directed up and not down at your feet), and slide on your toe-side edge.
4. Shift your eyes downhill, and follow in that direction with your body, legs, and board until you are horizontal on the hill, riding on your heel-side edge.
5. Look back uphill, and bring your body, legs, and board in that direction, turning onto your toe-side edge.
6. Repeat, and you'll be linking turns!

180

Learning to spin can be at least as terrifying as getting on a snowboard and taking off down the hill for your first time. You will definitely feel some nerves and adrenaline. But that's what you're doing this for, right—the adrenaline rush? Willingly jumping and twisting your body into the air and attempting to land smoothly may seem irrational, but not only is it possible, it is thrilling. If you've been studying videos and watching other people on the mountain, then you're one step ahead of the game.

As we've mentioned before and will mention again, visualization is a huge part of snowboarding and landing tricks. You must see yourself perform a trick in order to actually accomplish it. If you focus on falling or hurting yourself, then that is likely what is going to happen. Instead, think about how what you are trying to do is absolutely possible and how physically capable you are. Picture yourself jumping off the ground, spinning your body perfectly, stomping the trick, and riding away feeling happy. Visualize all elements of the trick, first slowly and step by step, then in real time in the actual setting, with perfect form and execution.

There are two types of 180s—frontside and backside. For frontside spins, you spin downhill, which means you can see where you are going and where you are landing throughout the spin. These are typically easier and less scary to learn for beginners than spinning backside and uphill and being blind to the landing spot.

FRONTSIDE 180

Visualize yourself spinning frontside first in order to get the motion and general idea in place. Just as when you first learned how to snowboard, you want to work your way from your head down, looking first in the direction you want to go and letting your body follow.

The number one thing people do wrong when they try to spin is getting scared during the motion and simply stopping midspin. This can get you injured. Committing fully to the trick, no matter what it is, helps you perform it successfully. As you progress to the more complex tricks described in chapter 8 and continue to develop your own repertoire, you may reach a point where you can tell when a trick isn't going as it should—by then your knowledge will be such that you can identify if and when you might want to bail. But at this point, a full and flat-out commitment is the safest approach.

To attempt a frontside 180, you are going to combine the ollie with a half turn while you're airborne and land the trick switch. If you've been practicing ollies and riding switch, it's just a matter of adding the turn. It's best to try your first 180 on flat ground or on a very small jump. Doing it for the first time on flat ground calls for a little more effort to pop into the air, but it's less scary and less dangerous than spinning off a jump. Doing a 180 on a jump, however, helps you pop and makes it easier to spin in the air because you can use the momentum from the lip of the jump.

Standing in a riding stance with your front foot forward downhill, try a spin and feel what it's like to jump in the air and turn your body. Put your weight toward the front of the board, pressing down with your front foot and leaning forward. As you lift your knees and begin to pop in the air, look in the direction you want to go (left if you're regular, right if you're goofy). As you reach the peak of your pop, turn your body—shoulders, upper body, hips, and legs—landing on your back foot first and then quickly on the front, to end in the opposite stance. Once you get the hang of it, try the 180 on a small jump that you can hike several times over and over again.

A few pointers to remember when doing a 180: Never look down or at your feet. This will mess up your balance and throw you off-axis. Take it easy and stay focused. Keep your knees bent and high. Stiff legs will make spinning difficult and make for very bad style too. Practice, practice, practice, as always, then move on to backside 180s, grabs, and bigger and more technical spins.

FRONTSIDE 180 INSTRUCTIONS

1. Find a minijump, about 2 to 5 feet (.6 to 1.5 m) long.

2. Since you will hardly need any speed, don't start off by pointing it (not turning, just staying flat and trying to gain speed) from far away. If there are other riders, gauge where they are starting from, and watch where they land. A good rule of thumb is to start about four turns away from the lip of the jump. You don't want to think about *making* four turns into the jump, this is just a general way to measure the distance you should be taking. After some practice you will be able to feel if you are going into a jump too fast or too slow. It usually takes a few tries to hit your correct speed.

3. Begin to ride toward the jump on your usual side (either regular or goofy).

4. As you approach the lip, use your shoulders and arms, winding up with your front arm across your body and back arm swinging back to gain momentum, gearing up to spin your body.

5. Right before the lip, ollie off of your heels, off of the tail of your board, and begin to turn your head to the left (if you're regular; turn it to the right if you ride goofy) toward the other side of the mountain. Using the momentum of your upper body, turn and open your front shoulder, followed by your back, opening up and looking to your landing. Bring the back shoulder all the way around to the front so you are facing the other side of the mountain.

6. Keep your knees bent, and quickly turn the rest of your body toward the other side of the mountain, continuing to look in the direction you want to go.

7. Land on your opposite toe-side edge, back foot first, and ride away switch.

BACKSIDE 180

After you have the feel for frontside 180s and can do them consistently, try doing them in the opposite direction using the directions that follow. For switch spins, the same rules apply, but follow your opposite foot forward.

BACKSIDE 180 INSTRUCTIONS

1. Find a minijump, about 2 to 5 feet (.6 to 1.5 m) long.

2. Since you will hardly need any speed, don't start off by pointing it from far away. See where other riders are starting from, and use the general four turns rule, although you may not need to make that many turns depending on how you feel approaching the jump.

3. Begin to ride toward the jump on your usual side (either regular or goofy).

4. As you approach the lip, use your shoulders and arms, winding up with your back arm across your body and front arm swinging downhill to gain momentum, gearing up to spin your body.

5. Right before the lip, ollie off of your toes, off of the tail of your board, and begin to turn your head to the right (if you're regular; turn it to the left if you ride goofy), toward the other side of the mountain. Using the momentum of your upper body, turn and open your front shoulder, followed by your back, opening up uphill and looking to your landing. Bring the front shoulder all the way around to the front so you are facing the other side of the mountain.

6. Because you are looking back uphill, over your shoulder, you may not be able to spot your landing until you are spinning.

7. Keep your knees bent, and quickly turn the rest of your body to the other side of the mountain, continuing to look in the direction you want to go.

8. Land on your opposite heel-side edge, back foot first, and ride away switch.

Grabs

Now that you can jump and have begun to spin, it's time for you to learn how to put some style into it. You don't want to be flailing all over while you're up in the air. Establishing control and making what you're doing look cool and natural identifies you as a solid snowboarder. Grabs let you demonstrate your skills and change up a trick to give it some oomph. Being able to do them properly will also help you maintain control when you start attempting more technical spins. Every grab has an endless number of variations. A rider can perform a grab along any part of the board, toe or heel-side, nose or tail and can grab with one or even both hands in endless positions. Riders add grabs to personalize a trick and add more style. Nail down the basic grabs presented in this section, then tweak them on your own. Always remember to stay bent when attempting any grab, and for a clean grab, wrap your hand around the edge of the board.

You can also do a double grab. The double has many variations, but it's any grab (front, back, toe, or heel) performed with both hands. Both hands will be grabbing the edge of the board, whether it's both grabbing the nose, both grabbing the tail, one grabbing either, or even crossing your arms and grabbing (if you are skilled); there are many ways to get creative with a double grab. Grabbing with the leading hand in between the back bindings on the heel-side edge and the back hand between the frontside toe-side edge is a common double grab. You can add in a spin once you get your grabs dialed, although performing double nose or tail grabs is more advanced, since positioning your body in that way may feel strange and can throw off your rotation. Pick a style and try it out for yourself.

INDY GRAB

The indy grab consists of grabbing the middle of your board with your back hand on the toe-side edge in between your feet. Practice on flat ground by bending your knees and reaching down with your front hand directly between your legs. When you're ready to try it in the air, grab in between your feet at your toes with your back hand as you start to peak in the air, right off the lip. Hold the grab until you start to come down from your jump. There are a number of things you can do with your other arm, but most riders throw it in the air during the grab, either naturally to help with balance or for style.

INDY GRAB INSTRUCTIONS

1. Ride toward a small jump, staying low and bending your knees.
2. As you approach the lip, pop an ollie in the air.
3. The more deeply bent you are the better. As you peak in the air, reach down (but don't look down; it should be a natural motion) with your back hand in between your feet on the toe-side edge of your board, keeping your grabbing arm bent.
4. As you descend, let go and land with your back foot flat on the snow, followed by your front.
5. Ride away and try it again.

METHOD GRAB

The method grab is one of the most talked about and sought-after grabs in snowboarding. The method takes considerable time to perfect and tweak out, and there is a lot of controversy about how to do it properly and who does it best. This trick has been celebrated in its own contests and events in recent years. Most riders consider the method the epitome of snowboard style. The method takes superior skill because you need to move the board and your body while in the air.

To attempt a method, ollie and pop in the air, lifting the board behind your back. This sounds really odd, but it's almost as if you are jumping in the air and bending both your knees toward your butt. When the board is in the air behind you, grab the heel-edge center of the board with your front hand. Most riders throw the opposite hand up in the sky. The entire time your whole upper body is facing uphill, but your shoulders and head are tweaked downhill. As you descend, release your hands and land as you normally would, and ride away downhill. The method seems unnatural at first, but it gets easier with practice, and the variations are fun and challenging. This trick is super fun and essential for all genuine snowboarders. Watching videos and seeing it in action will help you perfect yours.

METHOD GRAB INSTRUCTIONS

1. Ride toward a small jump, staying low and bending your knees.
2. As you approach the lip, pop an ollie in the air, lifting your knees toward your back and butt.
3. Your body should be facing uphill, except for your shoulders and head, which should be facing slightly downhill.
4. As you lift your knees toward your back, reach to the heel-side center of your board so your base, also known as the bottom of your board, is high in the air and at an angle.
5. As you descend, let go of your grab and bring your feet back underneath you so you can land with your back foot first, flat on the snow, followed by your front.
6. Ride away and try it again.

NOSE GRAB

All you want to do for a nose grab is grab the nose, or front of your board, with your lead hand. Grab at the actual nose, not the side edge of your board. As always, stay bent as you make the grab. Lean toward the nose to grab, but not so much that all your weight is forward. Find the point between leaning and keeping enough balance to control the spin and land properly. Release from the grab as you start to come down in the air. Put your other arm out to your side.

NOSE GRAB INSTRUCTIONS

1. Ride toward a small jump, staying low and bending your knees.
2. Ollie, popping off the lip of the jump and into the air.
3. As you reach the peak, reach to the nose, or front area, of your board.
4. Grab the front of the board where it curves, slightly toe-side, slightly heel-side, or dead center.
5. As you descend, let go and land with your back foot first, flat on the snow, followed by your front foot.
6. Ride away and try it again.

TAIL GRAB

For the tail grab, do the same thing as you did for the nose grab, but reverse it to the tail, or back area, of your board. One grab may come more naturally than the other, so try both and see how they feel. For the tail grab, reach for the tail end of your board with your back hand. You must grab the very back of the board where it curves, slightly toe-side, slightly heel-side, or dead center. Keeping your knees bent, reach back and grab where the tail arches at the very end. Practice using your weight distribution so you don't throw yourself off balance.

TAIL GRAB INSTRUCTIONS

1. Ride toward a small jump, staying low and bending your knees.
2. Ollie, popping off the lip of the jump and into the air.
3. As you reach the peak, reach toward the tail, or back area, of your board.
4. Grab the very back of your board where it curves.
5. As you descend, let go and land with your back foot first, flat on the snow, followed by your front foot.
6. Ride away and try it again.

CRAIL GRAB

Crail grabs are a stylish trick, mostly done while performing a straight air. It is pretty difficult to spin while grabbing crail. The crail grab resembles a cross-touch motion, similar to reaching down to your opposite foot, while standing on flat ground. Riders tweak the trick out by straightening their legs while in the air or bending just the front knee and straightening the arm they are grabbing with.

CRAIL GRAB INSTRUCTIONS

1. Find a small jump.
2. Ride toward the jump, staying low and bending your knees.
3. Approaching the lip, pop to ollie in the air.
4. The more bent you are the better. As you peak in the air, reach across the front of your body with your back arm, grabbing the toe edge in front of your front binding. Add some style by straightening your legs while in the air or bending just the front knee.
5. Straighten the arm you are grabbing with to properly perform the trick. Your front arm should naturally open up behind you.
6. As you descend, release from the grab, spotting your landing and landing with your back foot first, flat on the snow, followed by your front.
7. Ride away and try it again.

MUTE GRAB

Grabbing mute may seem easy since it is just grabbing in between your bindings with your leading hand, but there are a few tips to help you lock down this grab properly. It can actually be somewhat awkward because the grab can sometimes throw you off axis. Adding a mute grab to your arsenal of tricks will surely up your status, so make sure to keep those knees bent and stay centered. You can add a spin once you lock in the grab on a straight air.

MUTE GRAB INSTRUCTIONS

1. Find a small jump.
2. Ride toward the jump, staying low and bending your knees.
3. Approaching the lip, pop to ollie in the air.
4. Keeping your knees super bent and staying centered on the board, grab with your leading (front) arm in between your bindings on your toe-side edge right after you pop off the lip of the jump.
5. Do not lean forward since this may cause you to rotate. Lean back or stay centered low, and bend the arm you are grabbing with. Your opposite (back) arm will naturally fly back toward the tail of your board.
6. As you descend, release from the grab, spotting your landing and landing with your back foot first, flat on the snow, followed by your front.
7. Ride away and try it again.

Rail Tricks

Some people hate rails; others are obsessed with them. Locking in on a rail and being secure about what you are doing is an awesome accomplishment. Remember to watch videos and study live riders performing basic rail tricks first, rather than just diving into it. Knowing how to hit rails and jibs and becoming confident with it will come over time and with lots of practice. Your ollieing skills should be on lock by now, and riding a piece of metal or plastic is another adventure in your journey as a snowboarder.

The number one tip for attempting rails and jibs on your own is to always stay flat on your board. Never maneuver in a rail trick as if you are making a turn on your heel- or toe-side edge. You never want to carve or get on an edge of any sort on a rail unless you intentionally need to do so as part of the trick. Nearly all rail tricks require you to be flat-footed on your board. Most rail riders actually detune their edges with a file or grinder of sorts to make the metal edges of the board dull so they don't catch on the features. Depending on the features, a sharp edge can easily catch and throw you off if you aren't careful. Most edges dull on their own over time, but if you are getting into riding rails more, filing and detuning edges may be something to consider. So remember, always stay flat on your board, keep your knees bent, and stay loose when riding rails and jibs.

Start by learning some simple rail tricks on ride-on features. As you gain experience and confidence, you can ollie onto the rail.

50-50

The most basic and easiest rail trick is the 50-50. Ride your board in the exact position that you ride sideways down the hill: nose first, tail last. For your first attempt, try getting on a short ride-on flat box, if possible. Once you feel solid locking in 50-50s on a flat box, try a short, mellow, metal round rail, which you should be able to find in the same beginner park area where the ride-on flat boxes are located. The concept of attempting a 50-50 is identical; it will just take a little more balance and confidence since the feature is more advanced. That shouldn't be a problem, though, since you are practically a pro! When you are ready, you can take your 50-50 to a feature with a lip and gap, and ollie onto it to start the trick.

Watch where others are starting to drop from, and use the four turn rule if applicable. This will help you gauge the speed required to get onto the feature and to recognize if you need to go faster or slower. Never be ashamed to ride up to the feature and stop before you reach it. Sometimes you will just feel off as you approach, whether it's with your balance or speed. A lot of riders do this too to speed-check something before they attempt it. It's generally better to go too fast than too slow when approaching a rail or jib because the closer your board and body are to the fixture, the less time you have to react. This may sound strange, but trust that going too slow can actually make it more likely that you will catch on a feature and make it more difficult to ride to the end and execute the landing.

As you're riding up to the feature, look to the end of the box or rail, not down at your feet. Looking at the end of the feature, rather than looking at your feet or a different part of the feature, gives you a much better chance of landing well. The saying "Look where you want to go" absolutely applies on rails and jibs. Keep your body weight and position centered and low (not leaning forward or back) on your board, and keep the board completely flat. You don't have to make many movements—just ride straight onto the feature, nose first, tail last.

Stay bent and loose. Straightening and locking your knees will likely cause you to fall. Once you are on the feature, stay flat and centered on your board all the way to the end. Once your nose comes off the feature, look to your landing spot and ride away. Simple.

50-50 INSTRUCTIONS

1. Make sure you drop in far enough away to get some speed, but not too far away so as not to have control riding onto the feature. It's best to begin a little farther away and slow yourself down by carving, although you do not want to carve onto a feature ever, unless you want to fall.

2. Ride toward the feature as you would normally ride down the mountain, looking to the beginning of the feature where you are going to ride on. For a ride-on feature, stay flat (without an edge into the snow), and keep your knees bent in preparation for getting on the feature. For features with a lip or gap, load your weight on the tail end of the board and bend your knees to get ready to ollie.

3. Keep your nose facing downhill and your tail facing up as you ride or ollie onto the feature, staying low and centered on your board and looking to the end of the feature and not at your feet.

4. It's going to happen quickly, but remember to keep your board flat and not get anxious. You will be just fine. Stay calm and confident.

5. Look to the landing, and ollie or ride right off the feature and onto the snow, riding away.

BACKSIDE BOARDSLIDE

When you are feeling comfortable on rails, you can think about stepping up to frontside and backside boardslides. Try backside boardslides, also known simply as boardslides, first because in the frontside version you have to turn your body back and uphill, and just like spinning backside as opposed to front, the shift your body has to make for frontside boardslides is more difficult. During a backside boardslide, you turn your body 90 degrees to the front of the feature. As you turn to the front (even though the trick is named a backside), you open up your body downhill, as you would if you were spinning frontside, so that you are riding horizontally, making a T with your board on the feature.

Ride onto the feature with your toe side first and the tail following. On a rail, you want to ride toward the feature and approach as you would for a 50-50, but as you hit the start of the feature, open your body and board downhill so that both your nose and tail are off the feature. This may sound scary, but it is actually quite simple and fun. Keeping your knees well bent will help you balance throughout the trick. Riders also tend to balance with their arms out in a T position, as you would if you were walking a tightrope or walking on a wall. As you spot your landing and are almost at the end of the feature, start turning your body back into your normal stance so that by the time you hit the end, you are ready to ride away. Riders sometimes ride the whole feature on the boardslide and ollie off. While in the air, they turn their bodies back into their normal riding position (front foot pointed downhill), land, and ride away. When you are ready, you can pick a feature with a lip and gap, and ollie onto it to start your boardslide.

A B C

BACKSIDE BOARDSLIDE INSTRUCTIONS

1. Make sure you are far enough away to get some speed, but not so far away that you don't have control riding onto the feature.

2. Ride toward the feature as you would normally ride down the mountain, looking to the beginning of the feature you are going to ride onto. For a ride-on feature, stay flat (without an edge into the snow), and keep your knees bent in preparation for getting on the feature. Add an ollie to perform this trick on features with a lip and gap.

3. Begin to turn the nose of the board and your lower body to face downhill as you would for a heel-side turn. Keep your knees bent and the base flat, with your entire body and board open and facing downhill. You want to think of making a T on the feature so that just the space between your feet is on the feature. Your nose and tail should be off.

4. Look to the end of the feature, and spot your landing.

5. As you reach the end of the feature, turn your lower body and nose back to a 50-50 position (the same way you approached the feature). Ollie or ride right off the feature and onto the snow, riding away.

FRONTSIDE BOARDSLIDE

For the frontside boardslide, you are going to do the opposite of what you did in the backside version. You will start toward the feature the same way as for the backside version, but you turn only your lower body, legs, and feet back uphill. Keep your eyes and upper body facing downhill, and turn your legs uphill, with both the nose and tail off the rail (only the center of your board on the feature). Start the frontside slide with your back foot and tail of the board first. Get yourself positioned on the feature, forming a T. Come off the same way as for a backside boardslide, turning your legs back to the front and landing with your nose first. Turn your board back into your regular stance and ride away.

FRONTSIDE BOARDSLIDE INSTRUCTIONS

1. Make sure you are far enough away to get some speed, but not so far away that you don't have control riding onto the feature. It's best to begin a little farther away and slow yourself down by carving if necessary before you approach the feature.

2. Ride toward the feature as you would normally ride down the mountain, looking to the beginning of the feature you are going to ride onto. As you approach, stay flat (without an edge into the snow), and keep your knees bent in preparation for getting on the feature. Add an ollie to perform this trick on features with a lip and gap.

3. Begin to turn the nose of the board and your lower body to face uphill as you would for a toe-side turn. Keep your knees bent and your base flat, and keep your upper body facing downhill. All you are essentially doing is turning your front foot so both your feet are even on the slope; just make sure your front shoulder is open downhill and you are looking in that direction.

4. Always look to the end of the feature and spot your landing. This trick is easy to catch on your toe-side edge, so the more you stay low and flat on your board the better.

5. As you reach the end of the feature, turn your lower body and nose back to how you approached. Ollie or ride right off of the feature and onto the snow, riding away.

NOSE SLIDE

Once you get the hang of the basic rail tricks, you can begin to put a twist on them. For 50-50s you can ride onto the feature as you usually would, then simply press your weight onto either your front foot for a nose slide, bringing your tail off the rail, or onto your back foot for a tail slide, bringing your nose off the rail. Nose and tail slides are fun and good to practice on flat ground, just riding down the hill as you usually would. They are great tricks to test your balance too and usually difficult to mess up, unless you lean way too much and end up falling. Both nose slides and tail slides are stylish but simple tricks to add to your arsenal.

For a nose slide on a rail, ride on like you would for a 50-50. Once on the feature, press all your weight onto your front foot, bending your front knee deeply and lifting your back edge slightly off the feature. Always look to your landing, and when you are about to reach the end, straighten yourself out, back centered, and hop off the feature as usual.

To perform a nose slide on a regular rail with a lip and a gap, you will ride up, following all the steps you normally would, except you are going to add an ollie, hopping onto the rail instead of just sliding right on. Ride-on features are primarily made for getting to know the feeling of what it's like to be on a box, rail, or jib. Being able to ollie, land, balance, and slide onto the feature comes with time.

F   E   D

NOSE SLIDE INSTRUCTIONS

1. Make sure you are far enough away to get some speed, but not so far away that you don't have control riding onto the feature.

2. Ride toward the feature as you would normally ride down the mountain, looking to the beginning of the feature you are going to ride onto. As you approach, stay flat (without an edge into the snow), and keep your knees bent in preparation for getting on the feature. Add an ollie to perform this trick on features with a lip and gap.

3. This trick consists of putting your weight onto your front foot and pressing on the nose of your board. Think of doing a boardslide, but with only the tail of your board off the feature. Keep your body and legs open and facing downhill, but always pressing more on the front foot.

4. Look to the end of the feature, and spot your landing.

5. As you reach the end of the feature, turn your lower body and nose back to a 50-50 position (the same way you approached the feature), coming off of your front foot and recentering yourself so you can land smoothly.

6. Ollie or ride right off the feature and onto the snow, riding away.

TAIL SLIDE

For tail slides, simply ride on as you would normally for a 50-50. Once you are on the feature, lean on and bend your back leg, pressing on the tail of your board to lift your nose slightly off the feature. As you approach the landing, even your weight back to center and ride off the feature as you usually would.

For the tail slide, just like a nose slide, the only difference when doing the trick on a rail with a lip and gap is adding an ollie. Make sure you feel confident and secure performing the trick on a flat box or ride-on rail before moving up to a more advanced feature. What's great about nose and tail slides is that if you aren't feeling balanced or able to press on either the nose or tail well enough on the feature, you can always bring your foot down flat and ride as you would for a 50-50.

TAIL SLIDE INSTRUCTIONS

1. Make sure you are far enough away to get some speed, but not so far away that you don't have control riding onto the feature.

2. Ride toward the feature as you would normally ride down the mountain, looking to the beginning of the feature you are going to ride onto. As you approach, stay flat (without an edge into the snow), and keep your knees bent in preparation for getting on the feature. Add an ollie to perform this trick on features with a lip and gap.

3. This trick consists of putting your weight onto your back foot and pressing on the tail end of your board. Think of doing a boardslide, but with only the nose of your board off the feature. Keep your body and legs open and facing downhill. It's fun to tweak this trick and add your own style.

4. Look to the end of the feature, and spot your landing.

5. As you reach the end of the feature, turn your lower body and nose back to a 50-50 position (the same way you approached the feature), coming off of your back foot so you can land smoothly.

6. Ollie or ride right off of the feature and onto the snow, riding away.

Making Rail Tricks Your Own

The possibilities for doing variations of rail tricks are truly endless. Here we've explained the basic tricks on the more basic features; don't be afraid to step up to bigger, longer, more technical features. You will find you like some more than others, and it will be easier for you to do tricks and feel confident on certain features.

Remember to add the ollie to ride features with a lip and gap. This is where practicing that ollie really pays off, because knowing how to pop on and off will enhance your progression as a snowboarder tremendously. The world is yours for the taking, so think big. You've made it this far, and if you stay with it, you're only going to get better. Look for the tricks to get more technical in chapter 8.

Pipe Tricks

Learning tricks in the pipe requires a completely different approach to what you are used to with riding jumps, rails, and other jibs. Trying tricks in the pipe can be daunting, especially if there isn't access to a pipe at your mountain and you get the chance to ride only a few times a season. Most pipe jocks hone their skills on jumps and jibs, but ultimately they must practice in a pipe on a regular basis. If your access is limited, your chances of getting really good at it are slim. The pipe certainly isn't for everyone, but if you like the feeling of riding a wave and getting airborne, you'll like this type of snowboarding; put these two experiences together and you'll have an idea of what it's like to conquer tricks in the pipe.

Learning to ride pipe is intimidating. The anxiety and fear that come and go with learning to snowboard come back tenfold when you take on the pipe. Given the sheer size of pipes (up to 22-foot walls), the thought of even dropping into one may seem unwise and just plain scary. What makes snowboarding so much fun, though, is that there are so many options and aspects to explore. Becoming a multifaceted, well-rounded snowboarder is difficult, challenging, and even fun.

The pipe is a whole new experience, and the thrill starts with the first drop-in. Review the advice from chapter 6 on how to drop in and ride the walls of a pipe, then work on the following tricks. Being able to get height out of the pipe should be your first goal. Aim to air out a few feet, land, and ride away clean.

At first, one of the hardest things about riding the pipe is finding and maintaining your center of gravity. Rather than being centered on your board, you have to get used to maneuvering your body and board with the wall, or "riding the wall" as most riders call it. As with other snowboarding milestones, learning to ride the wall takes some time, but once you get it, you'll realize that all the time you spent was well worth it. The fun and freedom of riding the walls are just the beginning, though. Once you can do it and can get out of the pipe, both frontside and backside, you are ready to try some airs and spins.

You will most likely get the hang of one wall and be able to get frontside or backside airs easier than the other, just as you found it easier to ride toe- or heel-side when you first started snowboarding. The only difference with pipe is you need to be able to ride switch if you are riding only one wall, until you grasp the concept of turning back and forth in the pipe, toe- to heel-side. It's easiest to get the hang of riding just the wall (and not airing out) first because you will naturally turn your body 180 degrees back and forth down the pipe.

FRONTSIDE AND BACKSIDE AIR: PIPE

Spinning in the pipe will come naturally once you get the feeling of riding back and forth down the walls. On frontside airs your are spinning down the pipe, and on backside airs you are spinning up the pipe. All it takes is a slight shift and turn of your body, like you do on frontside and backside 180s on a jump. The difference is that riding away on the pipe wall feels more like riding a wave. You aren't landing straight, with your nose facing downhill; in the pipe your nose will be heading toward the opposite wall, gearing up for your next air.

The frontside air is performed off of the toe-side wall (regular-footers off the right wall, goofy-footers off the left). Practice frontside airs to get the feeling of getting air out of the pipe on your toe side. It is the basis for every other trick in the pipe on your toe-side wall.

The backside air is performed off of the heel-side wall (regular-footers off the left wall, goofy-footers off the right). Practicing backside airs will help you get used to catching air off of your heel-side wall, and it will help you progress to more advanced tricks.

For both the frontside and backside airs, using the momentum of the pipe wall and your body is key. Use your arms to balance and legs to pop you in the air. Pumping up and down the wall will help you gain more air out of the pipe, which is what you hope to accomplish.

FRONTSIDE AIR INSTRUCTIONS: PIPE

1. Drop in opposite the wall you are going to hit. Your body should be facing uphill, with your front shoulder and head facing the wall you are heading toward.

2. Ride down the wall slightly on your toe edge, gaining speed and momentum. As you come up the opposite wall, keep your knees bent and your eyes looking up the wall.

3. As you approach the lip, get ready to ollie and pop in the air, prespinning with your arms swinging across your body.

4. Pop off of your toes, off of the lip, and get airborne just as you would jump straight off a normal jump; use your momentum from your arms to fuel your lower body as you begin to shift your eyes downhill. Use your arms to balance if you wish, or grab to better control your body. Stay calm and in control while in the air as much as possible.

5. As you descend, spot your landing on the transition of the pipe wall so you are now on a heel-side turn stance facing downhill.

6. Land in the middle of the wall, not in the flat-bottom or on the lip. Land with your back foot first, front foot last, riding away on your heel-side edge toward the opposite wall, gearing up for a heel-side air or spin.

Frontside air: pipe

BACKSIDE AIR INSTRUCTIONS: PIPE

1. Drop in opposite the wall you are going to hit. Your body should be facing downhill, with your front shoulder and head facing the wall you are heading toward.

2. Ride down the wall slightly on your heel edge, gaining speed and momentum. Stay bent, and use your legs to pump the wall for speed. Begin using your arms to prespin as you do for a backside 180 on a jump.

3. As you approach the lip get ready to ollie and pop in the air; use your momentum from your arms to begin to turn in the air.

4. Pop off of your heels, off of the lip, and get airborne just as you would spin a 180 off a normal jump, turning your gaze up the pipe wall, followed by your arms and lower body. Use your arms to balance if you wish, or grab indy to better control your body. Stay calm and in control while in the air as much as possible.

5. As you descend, your body should be completely facing uphill as it would during a toe-side wall ride. Spot your landing.

6. Land in the middle of the wall, not in the flat-bottom or on the lip. Land with your back foot first, front foot last, riding away facing uphill on your toe-side edge toward the opposite wall.

Backside air: pipe

Moving Toward Mastery

Some tricks may not feel at all comfortable to you, while others may come almost naturally. Remember to keep watching videos and to watch other riders performing specific tricks, and practice as much as possible. If you are getting easily frustrated because you are unable to land a certain trick, take a break or wait it out. It's never helpful or enjoyable to get angry about snowboarding. Stay focused, visualize, and have fun. You will eventually be dialing in all the tricks in this chapter, getting more creative and putting your own twist on them. Pressure and frustration will not accelerate your progress. You've got this! If you decide you want even more of a challenge, you can get to work on the tricks in chapter 8.

Taking It to the Next Level

Reaching the level where you can spin with ease and try more complicated tricks is one of the most gratifying achievements in advanced snowboarding. If you find yourself hitting a wall (figuratively, that is), and what you've been doing starts to feel redundant, it's time to think bigger. Being able to challenge ourselves is one of the reasons we snowboard. This is when mind over matter and all those years of practicing and watching videos really start to pay off. The challenge is getting past the fear of falling and finding a way to attempt new tricks without being intimidated.

Finding an environment that is conducive to progressing is step one. Start small and work your way up in the minipark. Massive features can be deceiving, and if you aren't fully prepared, you can seriously injure yourself. When trying bigger spins on jumps, you will probably have to move up to a larger jump than what you're used to in order to have enough airtime to accomplish your spin. On jibs you will find ollie-on features with bigger gaps to the feature to be far more challenging. Pay attention to the small, medium, and large labels on the features. Watch others to get a feel for speed and what you need to do to hit the features. Start by straight-airing jumps you've never hit, and try the most basic moves on a rail before you move on to more technical tricks. In the pipe, if you're already getting the chapter 7 tricks down and you have a good feel for this style of riding, start to go bigger and try more advanced tricks.

Don't be scared. Remember, if you psych yourself out and think you can't do it, you make it more likely that you will fall. But don't feel compelled to do more than you feel ready for, either.

Even pros may never be able to accomplish every item on the ever-expanding list of possible tricks. There simply isn't enough time in the day, and all snowboarders have particular tricks they simply don't feel comfortable doing. So set your sights on whatever challenge appeals to you, and progress at your own pace.

Use the guidelines and step-by-step instructions that follow to decide what you want to do next. You can move through the spins from smaller to bigger, perfecting switch, front, and backside versions. You can put a twist on your arsenal of jibs and add more technical skills. Or maybe your goal is to smoothly ride switch, frontside, and backside on the features. Consider the tricks presented here as the beginning; once you master the most common tricks, you can throw in your own style and add some variety to set yourself apart. Following the guidelines to learn how to perform new tricks is exciting, but putting your own twist on them and discovering fun new ways to tweak a trick are what make them awesome.

To have even more fun as you develop your snowboarding skills, share the experience with friends. Riding with others who can show you new things or work with you to figure out tricks is extremely helpful. For most people, doing any activity with friends is more fun than going it alone, and practicing tricks in a group you are comfortable with can help you progress faster. Different members of the group will be better at particular tricks, so you can all teach, encourage, and learn from each other. Being in a group helps you keep your perspective, too—it reminds you not to take riding so seriously that you forget to have fun with it.

If you have the desire to expand your skill set and the dedication to stick with it, you will eventually reap the rewards. As with your snowboarding journey thus far, there will be easy times and hard times as you continue to progress. Some tricks will come more naturally than others. Harder, more technical tricks are naturally going to take more time to learn and land. The challenging nature of the sport just means there is always room to grow.

A few reminders: Visualize, visualize, visualize, and stay safe. Look before you leap. Watch others. Be aware of your surroundings, and know your boundaries. Always go from easy to hard and from small to big. Set a realistic pace. Make sure you can land each trick solidly time after time. Doing a trick once, or even a few times, doesn't mean you've learned it. If you move on too quickly, you won't fully master each trick. With tricks at this level, being sloppy is not cool, and it can be dangerous to move on to a more complicated trick if you aren't secure on the simpler stuff. Practice each trick until you really have it down, personalize it and make it your own, and then go for the next one. A key part of progressing in snowboarding is knowing when to not push it. If you really aren't feeling it, don't try to force it. Be confident, but know your capabilities and be safe. Take it one step at a time, and you'll get where you want to go.

Now get ready to soar because we're going to help you take your riding to the next level.

Airs and Spins

As we mentioned in chapter 7, spinning typically comes easier in one direction or the other. Just as riding regular or goofy is easier when you first start riding, you will feel more comfortable spinning either front- or backside. By now, you should know what you are more comfortable with, since you've already mastered 180s. If you haven't, you need to before moving on to more technical spins. At first, some riders find it more difficult to spin a 180 than a 360 because you are landing switch on 180s. But learning 180s gives you the feeling of spinning, which is crucial, and being comfortable with landing switch will come in handy when you move up to 540s.

As always, visualization reigns. Being able to see yourself land is the most important element of attempting to spin. Assuming you have dialed in your 180s, both regular and switch, and have determined which way feels most comfortable, the next step is to visualize yourself spinning, executing, and landing a 360. Easier said than done, yes—but keep thinking positively, and the process will be less daunting.

If you find yourself barely clearing the jump, you need a little more speed. And if you are landing at the bottom of the downslope, or "flats," you need to slow down.

Being able to reliably time your spins will come with practice. Jumps may vary from day to day depending on the conditions, and you yourself might be feeling energetic one day and sluggish the next, so expect some variation in your performance even if you are doing the spin in the same location. When you are first starting out, you can begin to dial in the timing of the spins by watching others, getting your prespin down, and getting a good pop off the lip. Some riders rotate 90 to almost 180 degrees during their prespin motion off of the lip to make sure they get their spin around. There is no formula that works perfectly for everyone, but using the prespin method, looking in the direction you want to go, and spotting your landing will help you complete the rotation. Just as with anything in snowboarding, the more you practice, the better and more comfortable you'll feel. Once you get the frontside 360 down, work on backside spinning, and then move on to bigger spins on bigger jumps.

More technical spins may come pretty easily once you've dialed 360s. What it really comes down to is mind control and how much you are willing to accomplish. Some riders may not want to try any bigger spins, which is just fine, while others may dream of landing inverted 14s. If you're looking to continue progressing, now that you've got the feeling of spinning and know what you're supposed to do, moving on to 540s, 720s, 900s, and 1080s is mostly a matter of practicing and fine-tuning your motion.

Being able to practice repeatedly on the same jump in good weather is certainly ideal, but snowboarding involves adaptation. Developing the ability to adjust to changing weather conditions and to reassess your speed if the jump has just been groomed or is now smaller or bigger will truly help you become a great snowboarder.

Never head straight to a jump and do your biggest spin. Take a lap or two, check out the jump and landing, watch other riders, then straight-line it once to see how it feels. Although small to medium jumps are good for learning 180s and 360s, in theory, the bigger the spin you're attempting, the bigger the jump you should be hitting. Most 40- to 50-foot (12 to 15 m) jumps (the distance you are going in the air) are suitable for most spins. It may be difficult to guess size, but by watching others you can better assess it.

Moving up to bigger spins is all about speed and commitment. Greater speed and reliable prespin momentum will give you what you need to complete the spin and land. Also, bigger jumps usually have poppier lips that make it easier to go bigger.

It's easy to overrotate and spin too much when trying bigger spins, or to get scared and stop midspin. Always visualize first and continue to picture yourself landing even during the spin. Remember that the spin is possible, and at this point it is simply mind over matter. You have the skills and knowledge.

Once you are in the air, remember to stay calm and spot your landing. Don't look down at your feet. Keep your head up, and look in the direction you want to go. The most common and dangerous mistake riders make when performing spins is freezing up in the air and not fully committing. Watch and visualize before you move up a step in spins. The biggest spins done thus far are 1440s (see table 8.1). It takes tons of practice not only to do a 1440 cleanly and with style but even just to attempt it.

Find a small minijump to practice on, just as you did with 180s. Before taking on any jump, watch the speed other riders are taking, and notice where they are dropping in from. Try straight airs and speed-check the jump, assessing how forgiving the landing is, before starting to spin bigger. Try 180s and see if you can get a feel for the speed and how to maneuver to spin bigger. When you understand the speed and the movements, it's time to go for it and attempt your first 360!

Your head and eyes should always lead and have the landing in sight. Riders sometimes freeze midspin and get scared they aren't going to land. As long as you are looking to your landing and are trying the trick on a mellow jump first, there's no need to panic. It's normal to be scared, but staying calm and continuing to commit to the trick will help you land safely, just as you visualized.

TABLE 8.1 SPIN CHART

180: half a rotation, spinning 180 degrees
360: one rotation, spinning a complete circle, 360 degrees around
540: one and a half rotations, spinning one and half times, 540 degrees around
720: two rotations, spinning two complete circles, 720 degrees around
900: two and a half rotations, spinning two and a half times, 900 degrees around
1080: three rotations, spinning three complete circles, 1,080 degrees
1260: three and a half rotations, spinning three and a half times, 1,260 degrees around
1440: four rotations, spinning four complete circles, 1,440 degrees around

FRONTSIDE AND BACKSIDE SPINS: 360 AND GREATER

We'll describe the frontside 360 first because it doesn't involve spinning blind and is therefore easier and less intimidating for most riders. For the frontside 360, start in a riding stance with your front foot forward downhill, and ride toward the lip of the jump. As you approach the lip, prepare your body by prespinning your arms and chest to build momentum. Swing your arms across your body in the opposite direction of the spin, bending and brining your front arm across your chest and nearly straightening your back arm behind you. This prepares your body to rotate and generates power to initiate the turn.

At the lip of the jump, swing your arms forward and begin your spin, opening up downhill with your upper body, followed by your lower body. Ollie and pop off the lip, lifting your knees and turning your head toward your lead foot. As you reach the peak of your jump, turn your shoulders, upper body, hips, and legs, working the spin from the head down. Land with your back foot and the back part of your board first. Make sure you land on the downslope of the jump and not on the deck—the flat area of the jump between the lip and the downslope.

Spinning backside is a more technical trick than spinning frontside, but some riders find it easier to spin in this direction. The same rules apply to backside spins as you prepare for the jump, except you will be preparing to spin in the opposite direction and opening up facing uphill. This means that you will be spinning blind for the first half of the trick. If you tend to under- or overrotate while spinning, use your body awareness and arms to stay compact and keep yourself upright.

Remember to never look down at your feet. Always keep your head up and your eyes looking in the direction you want to go. Keeping your knees tucked and relaxed in the air will also help you spin. If you have trouble midspin, just do what you can to keep your body upright and land safely. Remember, staying committed to the trick and not psyching yourself out is one of the most important rules.

Begin to add grabs when you feel comfortable. Grabs may actually help you with controlling your spin since you are more compact while grabbing. Have fun and play around, adding your own flavor and style to your spins.

For switch spins, you will perform the movements as described previously for both frontside and backside spins, but you will start with your opposite foot. Body awareness really comes into play with the bigger spins. Remember, you will need more speed to hit bigger jumps and spin more. As always, practice makes perfect, and getting frustrated won't help.

FRONTSIDE SPINS 360 AND GREATER INSTRUCTIONS

1. Find a jump you feel comfortable spinning 180s on and confident trying to spin more. Remember, generally the more you are spinning, the bigger the jump should be since you will need more airtime.

2. Make sure the jump and landing are clear, then begin to drop, riding on your regular side (either regular or goofy) toward the jump, gaining speed.

3. As you approach the lip, use your shoulders and arms for momentum to prespin, gearing up to spin your body.

4. Right before the lip, use your prespin momentum to maximize your spin, driving your energy forward and initiating the turn. Ollie off of your heels, off of the tail of

F   **E**   **D**   **C**

Frontside 360

your board, and begin to turn your head (to the left if you're regular, to the right if you ride goofy) toward the other side of the mountain.

5. Keep your knees bent and turn your body, working from the head down, always looking in the direction you want to go. For the 360 and multiples of 360, look to land in the same position you took off. For 540s and other spins that end in a half rotation, you will be landing on your opposite edge and riding away switch. It's essential to look in the direction you want to go and to know where your landing is. Begin to complete the rotation as you spot your landing.

6. Spot your landing by determining where you need to stop and land on the snow, looking down the mountain. Land on your tail and then your nose, back foot first, and ride away down the hill.

BACKSIDE SPINS 360 AND GREATER INSTRUCTIONS

1. Find a jump you feel comfortable spinning backside 180s on and confident trying to spin more. Remember, generally the more you are spinning, the bigger the jump should be since you will need more airtime.

2. Making sure the jump and landing are clear, begin to drop, riding on your regular side (left foot forward if you are regular, right foot forward if you are goofy) toward the jump, gaining speed.

3. As you approach the lip, use your shoulders and arms for momentum to prespin, gearing up to spin your body and make your rotation. Your arms should go across your body in the opposite direction you are about to spin. So for a backside rotation, your back arm will come across your body and your front arm will swing out to the side.

Backside 360

4. Right before the lip, move your arms back across your body in the direction you want to spin, ollie off of your heels, off of the tail of your board, and begin to turn your head (to the right if you are regular, to the left if you ride goofy) toward the other side of the mountain.

5. Keep your knees bent and turn the rest of your body, spinning blind, in a complete 360, looking in the direction you want to go the whole time. For 540s and other spins ending in a half rotation, you will be landing on your opposite edge and riding away switch.

6. Use your body awareness to spot your landing, looking down the mountain, and land back on your heel-side and then toe-side edge, back foot first, riding away just as you began.

BACK FLIP

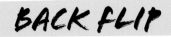

If thinking about attempting to spin on a snowboard messed with your head, thinking about getting inverted may simply be out of the question. But if spins leave you feeling hungry for more, flips may provide the adrenaline you crave. Spinning is almost an afterthought to landing a flip trick.

Back flips may seem and sound scary, but they are actually one of the easiest and least scary inverts to try. As with every other trick, try a back flip for your first time on a minijump. Being able to get the hang of this trick and land it on a trampoline or air bag with your board will help you learn to do it on snow. Once on snow, start in your regular riding stance, with your front foot forward downhill as you begin riding toward the lip of the jump and gaining speed. You will need a lot of pop off of the back tail of the board, so as you approach the lip, shift your weight toward the back in preparation for springing off the board. As you come to the lip, you should be looking up and positioning your body to flip. As you hit the jump, pop off the back of your board, tuck your legs, and try to stay as in control as possible. Look to the landing when you're halfway around, and visualize stomping your back foot and riding away. The trick is not to psych yourself out; once you have the momentum, your body will follow quickly and easily. Again, it's a feeling, and you may not land it your first try, but once you get the feeling of what you're supposed to be doing, it will become easier. The hardest part is always that first time.

FRONT FLIP

For the front flips, as with the back flip, getting the feeling on a trampoline or air bag first is helpful. Once on snow, start small once again. You are going to do the complete opposite of what you did for a backflip. Coming up to the jump, shift your weight forward in preparation for springing off the front nose of your board. As you hit the lip you should already be in position, ready to tuck and flip. For a front flip, you will be going in a direction that is unnatural for how the jump is built and flipping your body in a direction that feels uncomfortable. Knowing this from the start will take off some of the pressure of trying the trick. Once you reach the lip, bend your knees, using your shoulders and arms for momentum. This will be one of the only times you will need to look down while snowboarding. Pop off of the front of your board, tuck your head and body, and do a cartwheel-like spin, looking for the landing when you reach midflip. Even though you are tucking your head into your body, you should be able to see where you are going either to the left or right. Once you recognize the landing, visualize landing and try to stomp as much in the middle to the back of your board as possible. This will make riding away easier.

Rail Tricks

While learning tricks on rails, you will most likely experience a combination of highs and lows. Some tricks may and will come more easily than others. No matter what trick you are attempting, always wear protective gear—a helmet at the absolute minimum. Even if you've had a lot of practice, other factors may come into play, and you may have a whole other problem: The feature may be placed awkwardly in the ground, you may catch an edge, or another person may come into the scenario. Be aware of your surroundings, and follow the riders' code.

F

E

D

TAIL TAP

To tail-tap a feature, all you want to think about doing is tapping the feature with the tail end of your board. After completing a 50-50, boardslide, or variation, it's fun to add a little extra style with a tap of the board. Tail-tap as you ollie off a feature by moving your foot and angling the board in position, using your weight to gently tap with the tail of your board. It's a quick move, so visualize and know what you want to do going into the trick.

C   B   A

NOSE TAP

To nose-tap a feature, all you want to think about doing is tapping the feature with the front, or nose, of your board. After completing a 50-50, boardslide, or variation, it's fun to add a little extra style with a tap of the board. Nose-tap as you ollie off a feature

F   E   D

by moving your foot and angling the board in position, using your weight to gently tap with the nose of your board. Nose taps are often done by spinning off a feature because if you are riding 50-50 or boardsliding, it is more difficult to come around and tap with your front foot since it usually comes off the feature first. Keep this in mind, and watch others perform this trick and how they execute it before attempting.

WALL RIDE

Wall rides are a fun and challenging feature. They can be your best friend or your worst enemy. A wall ride is any feature that resembles a wall—a flat piece of metal, plastic, or something similar—coming up from the snow. They usually have a flat rail or box at the top to come up on and are sometimes built so you can slide or spin on top. A basic wall ride has a drop-in and some transition to use to gain speed so you can ride up the wall. The simplest way to ride a wall is to come up the wall straight (with your nose first, tail last), stall, and ride down switch. Think of a pendulum. You can also ride a wall like you would the wall of a pipe, coming up the wall as you would normally but turning your body 180 degrees on the wall, landing back, and riding away as you rode on. You should keep your board completely flat when coming up onto a wall and stay flat throughout the trick. It's easy to catch an edge on the wall and fall. Staying flat throughout the ride will help you land the trick. Then it is just a matter of body awareness and skill.

WALL RIDE INSTRUCTIONS

1. Watch others attempting the wall ride to judge speed first.
2. Make sure there is no one on or around the wall ride that may cause danger.
3. Once clear, proceed with your front foot first as you would for riding down the mountain normally.
4. Stay low and centered on your board, and prepare your board completely flat before reaching the wall.
5. As you approach, shift your weight forward, more onto your nose, keeping those knees bent and looking to the top of the wall, keeping your board flat the entire time. You are trying to reach the top of the wall, but you may or may not depending on your speed.
6. As you begin to feel yourself descend and make your way back down, look to the bottom or landing of the wall, shifting your upper body in that direction.
7. Stay leaning back on your tail now (you will be riding off switch).
8. As you reach the bottom of the wall, recenter yourself and keep your board flat until you are completely off of the wall and riding away.

Gap to wall rides are a newer challenging trick. Some resort parks have a lip on either side of a wall ride. You want to build speed as you would for a jump and then jump across the gap until you reach the wall ride, ride down it, and land. Ride away on the transition of the wall. This is an advanced trick since you have to be good at measuring your distance from the gap to the wall, so make sure you are comfortable riding regular wall rides. Have a specific trick in mind beforehand, and visualize your approach and execution.

This is just one example of many variations of hitting a gap to wall ride. Once you have it down, knowing the speed and landing, try different ways of spinning on the wall and coming into the wall switch.

Pipe Tricks

Gearing up and going for more advanced pipe tricks should be a natural progression if you are already able to complete the maneuvers explained in previous chapters. Mentally, it's even more important to stay focused when trying more complex tricks. Physically, you should be realistic about what you are already able to do and take your time working your way up. At this point, body awareness on snow should come pretty naturally. If you know you have the skills and you feel ready, then the next step is to try.

FRONTSIDE AND BACKSIDE SPINS 360 AND GREATER: PIPE

Performing bigger spins in the pipe means being able to get more air and have more control. Trying more technical spins is similar to learning them on a slope course, except you usually know what to expect every time since each wall is the same size and the landing is the same. The biggest difference will be the snow conditions from day to day and the change in the pipe throughout the day.

Once you get the frontside and backside airs (described in chapter 7) dialed, progress to a full 360 and continue up the cycle as you wish. The thing about spins in the pipe is that you are spinning slightly corked rather than flat because you are coming up off of the wall, turning, and landing down the wall. It sounds awkward and difficult, but it will come with practice once you get the hang of riding the walls.

Some riders can spin on the first hit, but when practicing and learning new spins, it might be easier to get some momentum down the pipe on a few walls and then try to spin. It's a matter of feeling it out and preference, but it's something to consider.

As opposed to regular jumps, spinning in the pipe gets more technical since spinning a 360, 720, or 1080 lands you back around to where you started but has you riding away switch. It will take a little time to grasp the concept, but once you've tried it a few times, and if you are already good at riding switch, you will get the hang of it.

The bigger you want to spin, the more pop and momentum you are going to need off the wall. Once you lose momentum, it may be hard to get it back. Come in strong and confident. Remember to visualize, watch others, and stay focused. Don't get angry. Practice and know that it is possible. If you aren't getting a spin you want, give it a day or two and try again. Don't put too much pressure on yourself. Sometimes it takes a little time to just click. And it will if you practice enough. You've got this!

Frontside spins are performed off the toe-side wall (for regular-footers off the right wall, goofy-footers off the left). Backside spins are performed off the heel-side wall (for regular-footers off the left wall, goofy-footers off the right).

Just as on frontside spins, for backside 360s, 720s, 1080s, and 1440s, you will be landing switch, so getting backside airs dialed and then spinning right to 5s might be easier. If you're already decent at riding switch, then chances are you should be good to go with spinning backside 3s and so on.

To spin switch, follow the rules for your switch side and test your skills. The variations are endless. Although it is possible to spin frontside and backside off the opposite walls as explained already (spinning backside off your toe-side wall or frontside off your heel-side wall), the best thing is to practice the standard format and make sure you are confident and secure spinning in all directions before trying to get more technical.

FRONTSIDE SPINS 360 AND GREATER INSTRUCTIONS: PIPE

1. Drop in opposite the wall you are going to hit. Your body should be facing uphill, with your front shoulder and head facing the wall you are heading toward.

2. Ride down the wall slightly on your toe edge, gaining speed and momentum.

3. As you come up the opposite wall, keep your knees bent and your eyes looking up the wall. Begin to prespin with your arms to help initiate the turn.

4. As you approach the lip, get ready to pop off your toes and into the air, staying low and keeping your knees bent. Use your prespin momentum to propel yourself up and off the wall to achieve the degree of spin you wish. (The bigger the spin, the more momentum and motion you are going to want to make with your body off the wall.)

5. As you pop, look and begin to turn your body in the air, opening up your body down the pipe toward your heel-side wall. For 360s, look back up the pipe and

Frontside 360: pipe

toward the wall where you initiated the turn to spot your landing. For 540s and beyond, you will need more momentum and airtime off the wall, so adjust your speed accordingly. For each spin, you are turning into yourself, with your upper body followed by your lower, and staying as compact and in control as possible.

6. Always look in the direction you want to go (left for regular footers, right for goofy riders) and not down at your board or feet. Look over your shoulder as if you are doing a pirouette in the air.

7. As you descend, spot your landing, with your body opening up the pipe if you are landing a 360, 720, or 1080 and down the pipe if you are landing a 540, 900, or 1260.

8. Land in the middle of the wall, back foot first, weight centered toward the back of the board to help balance yourself on the wall.

9. Ride into the opposite wall on your heel or toe side depending on what you landed.

Frontside 540: pipe

BACKSIDE SPINS 360 AND GREATER INSTRUCTIONS: PIPE

1. Drop in opposite the wall you are going to hit. Your body should be facing down-hill, with your front shoulder and head facing the wall you are heading toward.

2. Ride down the wall slightly on your heel edge, gaining speed and momentum.

3. As you come up the opposite wall, keep your knees bent and your eyes looking up the wall. Begin to prespin with your arms forward to help initiate the turn you will be making.

4. As you approach the lip, get ready to pop off your heels and into the air, staying low and keeping your knees bent. Use your prespin momentum to propel yourself up and off the wall to achieve the degree of spin you wish. (The bigger the spin, the more momentum and motion you are going to want to make with your body off the wall.)

5. As you pop, look and begin to turn your body in the air. Look in the opposite direction behind your back shoulder, turning your body back uphill. For 360s, look back down the pipe and toward the wall where you initiated the turn to spot your landing. For 540s and beyond, you will need more momentum and airtime off the wall, so adjust your speed accordingly. For each spin, you are turning out and opening up, with your upper body followed by your lower body, and staying as compact and in control as possible.

6. Always look in the direction you want to go (left for regular footers, right for goofy riders) and not down at your board or feet. Look over your shoulder as if you are doing a pirouette in the air.

7. As you descend, spot your landing, with your entire body and board opened up as if you are sliding on your heel side down the pipe if you are landing a 360, 720, or 1080 and facing up the pipe if you are landing a 540, 900, or 1260.

8. Land in the middle of the wall, back foot first and with your weight centered toward the back of the board to help balance yourself on the wall.

9. Ride into the opposite wall on your heel or toe side depending on what you landed.

Backside 540: pipe

HANDPLANT

Ahandplant is a trick you can do in just about any snowboard scenario. You can perform it on flat ground, on the wall or deck of the pipe, on a rail or wall ride, or in a quarterpipe or spine. Once you have the movement down, it's a fun trick to try in all different disciplines.

The handplant is mainly about weight distribution. You aren't actually holding yourself up with one hand; you are just making it look as if you are. To make learning this trick easier, we will describe how to do it on a small quarterpipe because the type of transition and shape of the pipe will help you succeed.

Think of doing a reverse cartwheel when attempting a handplant. Staying back on the tail of your board will help you plant your hand. Try not to lean forward, and remember to look down the transition instead of up as you perform the plant.

A   B   C

HANDPLANT INSTRUCTIONS

1. Find a small to medium quarterpipe with a smooth run-in and transition. Speed-check first and watch others before attempting.
2. Once the run-in and landing are clear, proceed to ride toward the feature as you would for a backside air.
3. Keeping your knees bent and remaining in control, approach the lip, transferring your weight to your back foot and the tail of your board.
4. Pop off the lip, and as your board goes in the air, reach your hand down underneath you onto the snow.
5. Keep your eyes looking down the landing, where you just rode up, to prevent sending yourself off-axis.
6. Bring your knees into your chest so your board is facing the sky and your arm touching the snow is locked straight, holding you in the air.
7. Add in a grab to obtain better control while you hold the handplant.
8. Drift your board back underneath you, in the opposite way you brought it up, swinging it back down onto the snow. You will be riding away switch.

Specialty Pipe Tricks

Specialty tricks are performed by riders who are the most highly skilled in the sport. Most of these very advanced tricks are attempted in practice and performed in competition. Specialty tricks have an extremely high degree of difficulty and danger. It's important to evaluate your skill level beforehand and be sure you are ready to try these tricks. Some professionals may never be able to land some of these tricks. Take everything in stride, watch others, and get a coach to walk you through the motions, if possible, so you understand the correct technique and know exactly what to do.

HAAKON FLIP

Named after legendary snowboarder Terje Haakonsen, Haakon flips are a switch frontside spin with a nose or indy grab and a relative straightening of the legs. You'll be dropping into the trick switch on your toe-side wall and spinning frontside, grabbing indy with your left hand while inverted. The grab and tweaking out the legs are the main parts of this trick. Being able to ride your switch walls well is also key. Perfect riding and spinning switch on your toe-side walls first, then begin to add the grab and straighten the legs as much as possible.

HAAKON FLIP 360 INSTRUCTIONS

1. Drop in switch on your toe-side wall facing uphill.
2. Ride toward the wall, gaining momentum and initiating a prespin for a frontside rotation.
3. Riding up to the lip, shift your momentum forward with the energy from your prespin and get ready to pop off the wall.
4. Begin to spin frontside as you would normally, looking in the direction you want to go and keeping your board underneath you.
5. While inverted, grab indy with your left hand, toss the other arm above your head for balance, and straighten your legs as much as possible.
6. Spotting your landing, hold the grab for as long as possible until you are descending.

7. Once you see the lip and transition, let go of your grab, bend your legs, and spot where you want to land, completing the 180 and landing on your toe-side wall facing the other direction.

8. Ride toward your opposite toe-side wall, riding away as you normally would.

CRIPPLER

To perform a crippler, being able to land 540s and beyond is a must. A crippler is generally an inverted frontside 540, 720, or 900 with a back flip or inverted flip at the end. Try frontside cripplers first off your toe-side wall, since this is the easiest way to try the trick. Once you get the frontside down, you can try the variations. For this trick you don't need a ton of momentum from your prespin. Use the wall and your speed to initiate and complete the trick.

CRIPPLER INSTRUCTIONS

1. Dropping in off your toe-side wall, stay centered on your board with your knees bent, looking up the wall you are heading toward.

2. Prespin to a degree as you approach the lip, but don't get crazy in generating momentum here because the pop off the wall and initiation of the spin will help you achieve it. If you are attempting a crippler 7 or 9 you may need to prespin a little more, but locking down the 5 first will help you feel it out.

3. Staying on your toes, begin to pop off the lip, waiting to spin until your back foot is on the lip so you don't spin off-axis and hit the deck.

4. Look over your back shoulder, and begin to spin as you would for a 540 or beyond, except you want to tuck your front shoulder across your body to get the inversion. Grabbing with the back hand as you reach the air will help stabilize you. Use your other arm for balance and to lead you around to your landing.

5. Complete the crippler by staying tucked and completing the last 180 of the spin, landing downhill on your heel-side wall for 540s and 900s and back on your toes for 720s.

6. Ride into the opposite wall on your heel or toe side depending on what you landed.

AIR TO FAKIE

Air to fakie is another stylish trick that is cool to learn. An air to fakie is basically getting air off of a hit, pausing (or sucking up your knees in the air), and rotating 180 degrees so you land and ride away switch. It's more or less a frontside or backside air, just with an added pause and "fake out" in between. You stop the trick midspin as if you are going to spin back the other way, but you continue the trick and land. This trick can also be performed on regular jumps. It isn't just a pipe trick.

FRONTSIDE AIR TO FAKIE INSTRUCTIONS

1. Drop in on your toe-side wall, gaining speed toward the opposite wall.
2. Look up the lip, staying low and gearing up to do a small spin. You won't need much momentum since the wall will help initiate your turn.
3. Keep your weight shifted on your back foot, pressing into the toe-side edge of your board. Start to twist your shoulders and hips as you would for a frontside spin.
4. Pop off the lip, staying compact and using your hips to slow you down in the air to make it look as if you may turn back the other way. Achieve this by keeping your shoulders in the direction you want to go but your hips back as if they are stopped in midrotation.
5. Spot your landing over your back shoulder, and bring your lower body the rest of the way around to complete the 180. Your board should remain underneath you throughout the trick. There shouldn't be any type of invert.
6. Land down the transition, and ride away switch on the toe-side wall.

ALLEY-OOP

Like almost every trick in snowboarding, the alley-oop has several different versions. The trick is any rotation in the pipe 180 degrees or more. A frontside alley-oop is a frontside air rotating up the wall instead of down. You are basically traveling in one direction while rotating in the other. You want to learn solid backside airs before you start trying the frontside alley-oop. When attempting this trick, you should approach the wall slightly on your heels as if you were going for a backside air.

FRONTSIDE ALLEY-OOP 180 INSTRUCTIONS

1. Drop in down the wall on your heel-side edge.
2. Ride toward the wall, gaining speed as you ride through the transition toward the lip. Look to the lip, staying back slightly on the tail of your board and heel-side edge.

3. Pop off the lip as you would for a backside air. Once in the air, grab in a style and location that you are familiar and comfortable with, to help stay in control and maintain balance for the remainder of the trick.

4. Rotate this trick slowly to remain in control and get a grasp on the feel of the rotation. As you are rotating, keep your weight centered, and look for the top of the landing as you begin to come around. All you are rotating is 180 degrees up the wall and around to face uphill on your toe-side edge.

5. Slow your rotation by slowing your head and upper body, which should slow the rest of your body in the air too. This will help you catch the transition and land flat-based. Come around slightly onto your toe edge.

6. Land in the middle of the pipe wall, and ride away on your toe side toward the opposite wall facing uphill.

MICHALCHUK

Invented by ex-pro Michael Michalchuk in the early days of snowboarding, the Michalchuk is a back flip or inverted under flip with a 540 rotation. There are a number of variations, but mainly you want to be able to spin 540s and do back flips. It should always be performed off of the backside wall.

BACKSIDE MICHALCHUK INSTRUCTIONS

1. Drop into the pipe on your heel-side edge, preparing to spin a backside rotation. Ride toward the lip on your heels, with your weight shifted on the tail of your board as you come up the wall. This will help you pop off.

2. Look up the wall and to the lip as you pop off the wall, looking over your back shoulder. Tuck your legs and grab to help with the flip and rotation. You will be blind until you come around 360 degrees halfway through the back flip.

3. Once the back flip is complete, finish the rotation by bringing the board back under you and spinning to your toe-side wall.

4. Spot your landing as you're completing your spin, and land in the middle of the wall, riding toward your toe-side wall.

Taking Your Skills Even Further

Keep in mind that the tricks in all the sections of this chapter are just the tip of the iceberg when it comes to what is possible on a snowboard. They will set the bar and give you a good starting point, but performing variations is where your skills will truly come into play. Each spin trick essentially has at least four variations: frontside, backside, switch frontside, and switch backside. Adding grabs, tweaking out a trick, and doing a front or back flip into or out of a trick are all other variations for the pipe, slope, and jibs. Getting down the basic trick front- or backside, depending on which one comes easier, then moving on from there and into testing your skills switch will make you a more well-rounded snowboarder.

The sky is truly the limit, so keep practicing and testing your skills.

CHAPTER 9

Getting the Most Out of Your Ride

Being fit for snowboarding has become a bigger aspect of the sport in recent years. Getting in shape during the preseason and sticking with it throughout the season help the pros stay competitive and avoid injury. Professional snowboarders have become true athletes, complete with trainers and workout regimes to prepare them for long, intense days on the hill. It's no small feat to get up on the hill and pull a winning run together. It takes a ton of training and practice to get a rider's body ready for competition.

But staying in shape isn't just for competitive snowboarders. Being fit can mean the difference between calling it quits midday and deciding to hit the backcountry for a few hours. Staying strong enough for the toughest hill and being able to take laps all day and not feel too tired and sore to do it again the next day are benefits any rider can appreciate.

Being able to ride longer and stronger will give you more time on the slopes and help you make the most of that time. Whatever your riding level, well-conditioned muscles perform better and resist injury better.

Any sort of athletic activity or exercise will help improve your snowboarding. Activities that are similar to snowboarding, or that use the same muscle groups, provide a more specific benefit.

Your legs and core are used most in snowboarding, so strengthening those muscles will increase your endurance and reduce your aches and pains. Squats and lunges, which you can do just about anywhere, are effective forms of exercise for building strong legs. Hiking in the snow, whether you're on a flat surface or walking uphill, provides an intense workout that challenges the legs and core. It's similar to running in the sand in that it taxes a variety of muscles to a much greater extent than performing the same movement on a solid surface.

Stand-up paddleboarding, which involves using a longboard to stand up and paddle on water, strengthens the legs and core and hones your balancing skills. Although the movements are different from those used in snowboarding, many of the same muscles are used.

Yoga helps you perfect and maintain your balance and provides a full-body workout. It also improves flexibility and helps you feel loose and in control of your body. Many riders use it before and after snowboarding.

For strengthening muscles and improving overall fitness, you can't beat light to medium weight training. It's a great way to strengthen your legs and core as well as your upper body (strong arm and upper-body muscles come in handy when you're pushing yourself up off the ground while learning new skills). As if that weren't enough, resistance training is good for the bones, and it speeds the metabolism.

Choose whichever type or types of exercise you find most appealing. If you like doing it, you'll do it more often and you'll stay with it. The important thing is to get fit and stay fit. Do your body a favor; if you want to live a long, active life and be able to ride for years to come, commit to an off-the-hill exercise regime. Your snowboarding will improve, and your body will thank you!

Snowboard-Specific Exercises

Most people know they have to work out to stay in shape for snowboarding but aren't sure what the best exercises are. Although an overall body workout program offers the most benefits, balancing exercises are especially important for snowboarders. If your time is limited, focus on exercises that promote balance.

As a rule, snowboarders don't go for spending long hours in the gym. Bodybuilding is not only incompatible with the freewheeling, outdoor-oriented snowboarding mind-set, it is in fact quite unnecessary. However, taking a little time to use weights or resistance bands to build lean, strong muscles is worthwhile because it will definitely pay off on the mountain.

To condition your body for the slopes, you have to put enough stress on the muscles to make them become stronger. The stress, whether it comes from weights or resistance bands, is what triggers the changes that make the muscles stronger. What this means is you need to challenge yourself and break a sweat. You should feel your muscles working, but in a good way. If you are going to put the time into working out, don't do it halfway—make a real effort. It will make you feel better, more confident, and stronger, day in and day out.

To make the process of getting stronger more fun and to keep yourself motivated, find a workout partner who snowboards. You can share your experiences and tips on different machines and exercises and talk snowboarding while you work out.

Remember, you should be looking for more reps at a lighter weight – not fewer reps at a heavier weight. Now, that doesn't mean that you should grab a weight that you are able to press 50 times. Find a weight that makes you work to achieve 10-15 reps. This light resistance will be much more effective for snowboarders than grabbing a weight that you can only complete 3-5 reps with.

Orthopedic surgeon Robert Marx out of New York, who specializes in shoulder and knee surgeries, recommends a variety of balancing exercises to prevent injuries. In a phone interview, Dr. Marx offered his opinion on what works for snowboard athletes. "There has been a lot of documentation to show that balancing really strengthens the muscles around the knee," says Marx. "Anything you can do to stand on one leg—squats, lunges, exercises on a balance board—is super important for staying strong." Balancing exercises, specifically any type of squats on one foot and lunges, help build strong muscles in the knees and make them more agile to take hard landings and long-term abuse.

Marx also recommends throwing an exercise ball or medicine ball against a wall, catching it as it bounces back, and squatting at the same time. This exercise is a good all-around body strengthener. Since shoulder injuries are just as common as knee injuries in snowboarding, Marx suggests keeping your upper body, back, and shoulders strong by working with weights and doing push-ups.

You don't need a lot of specialized equipment to stay in shape. Most pro snowboarders swear by foam rollers to stretch out their IT bands and backs. An exercise ball, a medicine ball, some light weights, a jump rope, and a variety of stretch bands are all cheap and simple products to keep at your home and travel with.

Some of our favorite core, upper-body, and lower-body exercises are described below.

Core Exercises

Your core helps you with balancing and maneuvering. Having a strong core is essential to staying up on your board and landing tricks. Include exercises for a strong core in your workout. Sit-ups and exercises performed on an exercise ball work the core and can be done anywhere.

Abdominal Crunches Using an Inflatable Balance Board

START

While lying on your back, place the balance board underneath the middle of your lower back. Your feet should be flat on the floor, legs together, and arms crossed in front of your chest.

MOVEMENT

Using the abdominals, lift your head, neck, and tops of your shoulder blades away from the floor. Slowly lower to the start position to complete one rep.

NOTES

To avoid putting pressure on your neck, be sure to keep your shoulders relaxed and your neck tucked in toward your chest while crunching up. Do not attempt this exercise on a wooden or hard-surface balance board. If you are having difficulty, place your hands behind your head or neck for support rather than crossing them in front of you.

Abdominal Roll-Out

START

Kneel on a mat or floor with your knees approximately hip-width apart. Grasp the ab wheel handles and position your arms directly beneath your shoulders. Keep your back flat and your abs engaged.

MOVEMENT

Roll the wheel straight out as you lower your hips toward the ground—your body should form a straight line from your shoulders to your knees. Using your abdominals, slowly roll the wheel back in until you reach the starting position.

NOTES

Roll only as far forward as you can while still maintaining good form. Do not allow the hips to drop toward the floor or the lower back to arch. If you are unable to return to the start position as explained, don't force it. Simply stop the rep and return to the start position.

Back Extension With an Exercise Ball

START

Begin standing close to a wall, facing away from it. Place the ball in front of you. Lie forward over the ball so that the ball is acting as a fulcrum point. The ball should be under your hips with your torso out in front. Put the soles of your feet flat on the wall behind you, with your toes firmly on the floor. Straighten your legs, keeping your weight distributed evenly between your feet and the ball. Place your hands behind your ears or across your chest.

MOVEMENT

Raise your torso up toward the wall as high as possible by bending backward at your hips. Hold for one to three counts. Slowly return to the starting position.

NOTES

Make sure the soles of your feet are flat against the wall and that your weight is pressed into the ball for stability.

Side Plank

START

Lie on your side and prop yourself up with your elbow. Your elbow should be positioned directly under your shoulder. All points along your body line should be straight, from the top of your head to your feet.

MOVEMENT

Brace your abs and lift your hips off the floor. As you lift your hips, imagine driving your elbow into the ground.

NOTES

In the final position, your hips should be lined up with your shoulders and ankles. Be sure that you do not bend at the hips. Keep your shoulders aligned vertically over your bottom elbow, and keep your bottom shoulder away from your ear on the same side.

Balancing Seated Twist With a Medicine Ball

START

Sit on the floor with feet firmly planted in front of you. Knees are bent, back is straight, and hands grip a medicine ball. With your elbows bent and tucked at your sides, hold the ball in front of your torso. Keep your back straight and lean back slowly until you feel your abs tighten. Then slowly lift your feet off the floor, being careful to maintain your balance.

MOVEMENT

Keeping a perfectly straight back with your abs pulled in tight, rotate your torso to the right as far as you can while maintaining good form. Return to the center. Repeat the same motion to the left and return to the center.

NOTES

Be sure to keep your back straight throughout all turns. Focus on the movement coming from the waist, allowing your upper body and arms to follow the twisting motion of the waist. Be sure that the twists are done at a slow pace to avoid injury. To make this more challenging, use a heavier weight or extend your arms straight out in front of you.

Upper-Body Exercises

Although most of the work in snowboarding is done by the core and lower body, the back, chest, and shoulders must be strong enough to withstand falls and get you on your feet again. Upper-body strength comes in very handy on major powder days or any time you get stuck in deep snow.

Power Push-Up

START

Start with your toes on the floor and your hands slightly more than shoulder-width apart. Look down at the floor to keep your head aligned with your body.

MOVEMENT

Slowly lower yourself to the floor, bending your elbows slightly back behind you. Your back should remain flat throughout the entire motion. Pause for a moment when you reach the lowest part of the movement and then begin to slowly push your body away from the floor while straightening your arms.

NOTES

If this is too difficult, you can start on your knees rather than your toes. Focus on performing this exercise slowly. You should be moving at no more than half the speed that you would for a normal push-up.

Chin-Up

START

Grab a pull-up bar with an overhand grip (palms facing away from you), with your hands just beyond shoulder-width apart. Your feet should not be touching the floor.

MOVEMENT

Without swinging or any other assisting motion, lift your entire body upward until your chin touches the bar. Slowly lower yourself back to the starting position. Complete as many reps as possible.

NOTES

It is important that you do not swing or use your legs to help you reach the bar. If you are having trouble, ask another individual to help. They should position their hands on your hips and provide assistance by lifting as you pull yourself up. Also, if you are using a bar that is low enough that your feet are touching the ground, bend your knees and cross your feet so you are not able to touch the ground.

Biceps Curl With a Resistance Band

START

Grab the handles and place your feet on the center of the band. Stand tall with your back straight, abs tightened, knees slightly bent, elbows tucked to your sides, arms extended down, and palms facing up.

MOVEMENT

Bend the elbows to curl your hands toward your shoulders. Slowly straighten the elbows to return to the starting position to complete one rep.

NOTES

Keep your back straight throughout the movement. The movement should only consist of bending at the elbows. If you need to lean or arch your back to raise the handles, use a band with less resistance.

Lower-Body Exercises

To balance your workout and build strong lower-body muscles and knees, since you are putting the most pressure on those muscle groups, include exercises for the lower body as well. Consider everything from your hamstrings and glutes to your calves when preparing an exercise program.

Lateral Lunge with Dumbbells

START

Grab a lightweight dumbbell in each hand and hold them to your sides with your palms facing your body. Stand with your arms relaxed and feet about six inches apart.

MOVEMENT

Slowly flex your hip and bend the knee of one leg until the knee is bent to about 90 degrees and your foot is off of the floor. Step to the side about three feet with this same leg and land softly on your foot. Straddle your opposite knee with each arm while keeping your head up and back straight. Sit back with the majority of your weight on the stationary leg. Keep your toes pointed straight ahead and both feet flat on the floor. Drive off the laterally extended leg and return to the start position. Repeat the same movement to the opposite side.

NOTES

Do not overstride on your lateral step. Work your way out slowly through trial and error. Keep your weight back and toward your heels; this will help you keep your knees in line with your ankles.

Forward Lunge With Dumbbells

START

Stand with your legs slightly apart and a dumbbell in each hand, with your palms facing in.

MOVEMENT

Take a big step forward while keeping your upper body as straight as possible. Lunge until the front thigh is parallel to the floor and the back knee approaches the floor. Push off and return to the starting position. Complete the same movement with the opposite leg to complete one rep.

NOTES

Make sure the forward knee does not cross the line of the toes.

Walking Lunge

START

Stand with your feet shoulder-width apart and your hands on your hips.

MOVEMENT

Take a big step forward and lower your torso until your back knee almost touches the ground. Knees should be bent at 90-degree angles. Push up, take another step, and again lower your torso. Continue to move forward, walking and lunging.

NOTES

To add to the level of difficulty, hold dumbbells in each hands. Complete the same movement, but allow your arms to hang at your sides throughout the motion.

Wall Squat With Dumbbells and a Ball

START

Place the ball between the wall and your lower back. Spread your feet shoulder-width apart and point your toes forward. Grasp the dumbbells, palms facing in, at your sides.

MOVEMENT

Slowly bend your knees to 90 degrees and hold for a three count. Slowly straighten your legs and return to the starting position, making sure to keep your knees bent slightly, to complete one rep.

NOTES

Place your feet far enough in front so that when you bend to 90 degrees, your knees don't go past your toes.

Leg Curl With an Exercise Ball

START

Lie on your back with your arms at your sides and your heels resting on top of an exercise ball. Keep your legs straight and toes pointing up.

MOVEMENT

Press your heels into the ball while raising your hips off the floor. Flex your knees and bring your heels in toward your buttocks while keeping your hips elevated. Return to the starting position by extending your knees slowly.

NOTES

Be careful not to press down into the floor with your head and neck. Make sure the hips remain elevated throughout the entire movement. If you'd like to add an extra degree of difficulty, try placing only one leg on the ball at a time.

Single-Leg Calf Raise

START

Stand on one foot, holding a moderately weighted dumbbell in your hand on the same side as the leg you have on the ground (right leg on the ground, dumbbell in your right hand).

MOVEMENT

Rise up on the ball of your foot at a slow and controlled speed. Once you have fully extended, return your heel to the floor. Repeat 20 to 30 times, then switch to the other leg.

NOTES

The weight of the dumbbell will be different for everybody. If you are unable to complete at least 20 reps, the dumbbell you are using is too heavy. If you complete 30 reps and feel as if you could continue without a rest, select a heavier weight for your next set.

Stretching

Stretching both before and after riding will most certainly help keep you flexible and loose. Yoga is always a good practice. It not only stretches your entire body but also helps you clear your mind and find your focus. Doing a short 5- to 10-minute stretching routine before you hit the hill will help you loosen up and get your blood flowing. No need to do a super intense stretch session. Stretching before the muscles are warmed up and pushing the muscles past the point of discomfort can actually cause injuries. Overstretching may also give you an inflated sense of ability. You may think your body is ready to take on anything from the very first run, when in fact it may still be digesting breakfast and waking up.

Before you begin any type of stretching routine, remember to get your heart rate going to elevate the blood flow. Something simple such as jumping jacks or a little jump rope will help raise that heart rate before you get into a quick stretch session. After you've finished a quick aerobic and stretch session, ride some small slopes and get the muscles working. Once you're finished, you're ready to stretch and hit some more challenging obstacles.

Stretching shortly after you finish riding feels good and improves flexibility. After relaxing for a few minutes, lie on your back and bring one leg at a time to the chest. Hold your knee with your hands locked for a few seconds. With the opposite hand, guide your knee across your body to stretch your hips. After you've done both sides a few times, pull both knees into the chest, making yourself into the smallest ball you can, and hold your neck into your chest. Hold for a handful of seconds and then release. This full-body stretch helps release tension in your muscles.

Following are descriptions of some of our favorite snowboard-specific stretches.

Advanced IT Band Stretch

START

Start in a push-up position on your hands and toes. Lift your right foot and slowly bend your leg so that your right knee moves toward your left hand and your knee and outer ankle rest on the floor. Slide your left leg back as far as comfortable, but keep your hips level and square to the floor.

MOVEMENT

Hold the stretch and push your hips toward the floor, keeping the back long, shoulders down, and chest lifted. Hold for 10 to 30 seconds and repeat the same movement with your left leg.

NOTES

This is an advanced, difficult stretch. If you are unable to keep the proper form throughout the entire movement, choose a different exercise, or you'll do more harm than good. If you are able to perform the stretch and would like to go for an even better stretch, fold forward and let your forearms rest on the floor in front of your leg.

Lying Hip and Glute Stretch

START

Lie on your back with your legs extended and your back straight (make sure to keep your lower back on the floor. Bend your right knee toward your chest while grabbing it with your left hand. Place your right hand out to the side.

MOVEMENT

Keeping your shoulder blades on the ground, use your left hand to pull your right knee across your body and toward the floor on your left side. Hold for 10 to 30 seconds and repeat the stretch with your left leg.

NOTES

You'll feel some discomfort during this stretch and that is normal. If you start to feel pain, that is a different story—stop! Don't bounce, and keep your shoulders on the ground at all times. You should never force your knee to the floor if your body does not allow it.

Wide-Leg Modified Forward Bend

START

Stand tall with your back straight, feet slightly more than hip-width apart, toes turned out, and your abs tight with your arms at your sides.

MOVEMENT

Keeping the legs straight and the abs tightened, slowly bend forward from the waist until your fingertips touch the floor, with your back in a flat position. If you are unable to touch the floor, just bend as far as possible. Think about reaching your chin out toward the floor in front of you. Hold for 10 to 30 seconds.

NOTES

Again, you will feel some discomfort, but if you feel actual pain, stop! Don't bounce, and if you can't reach the floor, don't force yourself to do so.

Single-Leg Toe Touch

START

Stand on one leg with a slight bend in the knee. Draw your shoulders back and keep your head in a neutral position (eyes level and chin parallel with the ground). Keep your non–weight-bearing leg in front of you with your hip and knee flexed. Keep your hands out in front of your body.

MOVEMENT

Bend forward at the hips with your back straight and head up. Extend your non–weight-bearing leg behind you while maintaining the flex in the knee. Reach down toward your toes, stopping about shin level. Return to the starting position by extending at the hips and bringing your non–weight-bearing leg forward again with the knee and hip flexed.

NOTES

Keep the back straight at all times while maintaining a slight natural curvature in your lower back. If you lose your balance, simply tap your non–weight-bearing foot to the floor until you are back under control. Never attempt to hop or swing your arms to regain your balance.

Myofascial Lower-Back Release

START

Sit on the floor with your knees bent, feet flat on the ground, and legs hip-width apart. Place a foam roller on the floor behind your back. Slowly lean back into the roller with your lower back as you place your elbows at a 90-degree angle directly underneath your shoulders. Keep the shoulders relaxed and away from the ears.

MOVEMENT

Shift your weight forward and back, allowing the foam roller to move up and down your lower back. Repeat several times.

NOTES

As you move the roller up and down by shifting your weight forward and back, search for tight and sore spots on your back and hold those positions to help decrease tension. You can also roll short passes over those tight areas to help relieve the tension.

Cardio and Endurance Training

Hiking is the go-to exercise snowboarders use to increase stamina and keep the leg muscles and knees strong. Professional snowboarders do a lot of climbing and uphill exercises. Running on flat ground is helpful, but hiking, biking, and climbing are better for the quads, which are heavily used during snowboarding. Hiking steep mountains and riding a road bike up and down hills are great endurance boosters.

If you don't live in the mountains, simply adjusting to the altitude is going to tax your endurance. Since the air is thinner at higher elevations, the same distance you usually go and activities you are able to do at sea level are going to become more difficult up high. Pushing yourself harder during the training you do at a lower elevation will help you cope better and have more stamina once you get to the slopes.

Some of the more popular cardio exercises or activities that can be great for snowboarders include running, swimming, jumping rope, aerobics, soccer, climbing stairs, and cycling. Choose cardio activities that you like to do and perform them at least 4-6 times per week for 30-60 minutes. Sessions that last longer than 30 minutes are necessary for building the endurance you need for snowboarding. If you haven't been cardio training regularly, start with fewer days and less time and gradually build up to 30-60 minutes.

Just because the snowboard season ends doesn't mean you should quit exercising. The average person rides only about six months out of the year, which leaves another six months for other activities. Doing some type of program, whether it's exchanging your snowboard for a surfboard and mixing in some regular weight training and balancing exercises or hiking and biking every chance you get, will help keep you in the workout mind-set. Change things up when you get bored, but keep moving. It's easy to get out of the habit of actively exercising, so make it a part of your daily routine. Remember that taking care of your body will help you become a better rider.

Whether it's riding bikes, running, swimming, skateboarding, wakeboarding, or anything in between, staying active and using your legs every day will pay off when it's time to hit the mountain. Hiking, climbing, and mountain biking are a few favorites of the pros, but many also follow a gym routine throughout the year. You don't have to work your legs as much as you would during a normal day on the slopes or run a marathon every day, but steadily building and maintaining strength and stamina are the keys to longevity on the slopes. And in the meantime, enjoy the mental clarity, energy, and overall sense of well-being that come with regular exercise.

CHAPTER 10

Competitive Riding

It takes a special breed of person to become a competitive snowboarder. In addition to talent, competition requires a deeper understanding and knowledge of the sport. Commitment and desire also differentiate those who ride for leisure and those who envision themselves on top of a podium. Competitive riders dedicate their lives to endless practicing and traveling. They are determined to go as far as their talent and effort will take them.

There are two levels of competing as a snowboarder. Riders start out on the amateur circuit and work their way through the ranks, gaining professional status over time, with a ton of hard work and some wins at high-profile contests.

Amateur contests are a great way to break into competing and determine if you are cut out for the big leagues. Some excellent riders simply don't like contests. They don't like being judged and being confined or restricted by a category or style of riding in order to win. If you are interested in the competitive world, trying out some amateur events will give you a chance to see what it's like.

There aren't many restrictions for entering amateur events. Organizers generally group competitors by age range and skill level. Finding events to enter is pretty simple. Visit resort websites to find out what is going on in your area and how to enter. Many events simply have you show up the day of and register. Even if you aren't sure you have what it takes or will even like competing, you really won't know until you try. You'll be competing against riders of similar age and ability, and you just might surprise yourself. If you are interested, give it a shot. Everyone has to start somewhere, and some very accomplished riders might never have learned how good they could be if they hadn't entered amateur competitions.

There are all kinds of amateur events, from slopestyle and pipe to rail jams and downhill. Amateur contests are a great way to find out what types of contests you enjoy. Most riders find a preference when competing as an amateur and begin to concentrate on one discipline in order to really master it.

Amateur contest winners may get only a few hundred dollars or sometimes just some gear. While some amateur riders may receive flow, just product and some endorsement from a brand, they are considered amateurs until they are signed as professionals.

Getting noticed by big-name contest organizers and big-time sponsors is the ultimate goal of riders who want to go pro. The best way to get noticed is to get out there and compete. Socialize with everyone at contests. As in other areas of life, part of getting to the next level is who you know and how you work your connections. Skill and talent are essential, but you have to put yourself out there in order to get anywhere.

Riders can't simply decide to enter events such as the X Games, the Burton U.S. Open Series, or the Winter Dew Tour; they must be invited. The U.S. Open Series is open to amateurs, but they must compete and win in rounds of pre-qualifiers before making it to the semifinals where some of the best riders in the world compete. Most professional competitions are on an invitation-only basis, and to qualify for such events, the riders must have won numerous ranked events or have performed well in qualifying competitions. Typically, the more contests you do, the better. Getting your name and face out there and showing that you can compete on a professional level, either by the tricks you do or by winning events, will get you invited to bigger events. There is no set path or strategy for reaching pro rider status. It takes a combination of effort, skill, and drive.

Big-name events have major sponsors that put up bigger prize purses for the winners. In pro events such as the X Games and U.S. Open, winners can take home upwards of $20,000.

Sponsor status is a defining feature of the professional circuit. Generally, once riders have been picked up and become sponsored by a brand on a professional level, their status turns to pro, and they are able to compete on this level. The biggest sponsorships are usually the board manufacturers. Locking in a contract with a board sponsor means you have reached a very high level and should be competing in the top pro contests.

Getting Started

Snowboard clubs through schools and resorts can help get you started on the amateur circuit. For free or a small yearly fee, you can travel with other riders, share your experiences with them, and prepare for riding in contests as a group.

Many riders join the United States of America Snowboard Association (USASA) if they are thinking more seriously about competing. The USASA is available in many regions of the United States. Check the website www.usasa.org to find out how to join. It's easy to get in, and there are different levels of commitment. Once you join, you are allowed to enter USASA events throughout the season, and if you score well you may be invited to nationals. Being invited to and winning nationals has launched the careers of many pro riders. Being a part of this influential organization will build your competition portfolio, help you learn the scoring system, and prepare you to win competitions.

Team managers and reps from companies attend smaller contests to headhunt and look for new talent. Performing well will usually get you noticed. If the right people notice your skills and see potential, you may be on the road to pro status.

Riders also put together reels showcasing their riding to provide to sponsors. Known as "sponsor me" tapes, riders send videos or online edits to team managers, who assess if they would like to sponsor them or not. Finding out who should be seeing the tapes and knowing where to send them is the hard part. The truth of the matter is, if you're standing out with your trick ability, style, and effort, you can generally find a way to get noticed by people who can help you.

For some, those who are very lucky and very skilled, becoming a professional competitor and gaining sufficient exposure to be invited to the major competitions may take only a few seasons of solid riding, the right exposure, and luck. For most, it takes many years to reach pro status. The reality is that very few actually reach pro level, and it can take a long time. But it isn't impossible of course. If becoming a professional big-name competitor is your number one goal, go for it. Join a snowboard team; become a member of the USASA (the majority of pro snowboarders get their start this way); and find a coach, through your school, resorts, friends, or colleagues, who can guide and support you.

Given the growth of the sport and the expanding number of competitors, if you don't start out at an early age and don't have the means to have a coach or team, it's especially tough to make a name for yourself. Coaches and teams help get your name out there, which opens the door to more opportunities. There are a ton of riders out there who are very good, and if you don't know how to sell yourself, then it's going to be a long road. Promoting yourself and what makes you stand out from everyone else is something that coaches and other professional riders can help you with. Some professional competitors are not universally considered to be among the best snowboarders, but because they market themselves well, on their own or with help, they appear at every big event and are always in the spotlight.

To become a top professional competitive snowboarder, you must be willing to live and breathe snowboarding. If you have other commitments, distractions, and interests that demand a great deal of your time, competing might not be for you.

Although snowboarding isn't a team sport, there is an element of camaraderie, and competitors often develop strong friendships with one another. Connecting with other riders helps you ride more, ride harder, and ride stronger. If you are on the same circuit, you can travel together and encourage each other. Although you compete on your own, having friends there to support you makes the overall experience more enjoyable.

Being a good sport to your fellow riders and giving credit where credit is due helps you bond with others. This bond will help you enjoy competing with and against other riders, and it will help you succeed and reach professional status. Other riders can make introductions and contacts for sponsorships and make you a better overall rider. Feeling you are among friends who understand the challenges you face and who support you elevates your performance.

Competition can be rough, even for very talented riders. It can sometimes be very difficult not to get upset by the setup, scoring, or judging when it does not sufficiently highlight or reflect your true ability. Try not to be too hard on yourself—remember that everyone struggles at times. Look at the bigger picture. Learn from your own experiences and those of other riders. There is no place for bad attitudes and anger in snowboarding. If these traits are a regular part of your snowboarding, then you are doing it for the wrong reasons and you need to adjust your perspective. If you stay humble and can win and lose with grace, class, and a smile on your face, you will gain respect from your peers. Think about why you ride. If money and fame are your main motivations, you are missing the point. If fame and fortune come your way, that's great, but put your focus on progressing in the sport you love and doing the best you can do. And don't forget to have a good time. Remember, snowboarding is supposed to be fun!

Preparing to Compete

To compete at your highest level, your body and mind must be fully prepared. To do your best, you must have a healthy body and a clear head as you begin competing. We talk in detail in other chapters about the importance of staying fit and training even in the off-season. As you progress in the world of snowboarding competitions, these courses of action go from being helpful to being absolutely necessary.

You can't afford to get out of shape during the year and then play catch-up before big contests. And you don't want to be sidelined with an injury that could have been prevented by doing strength and conditioning work. Developing the stamina to spend long hours training in tough conditions takes a consistent effort. Stay involved in physical activities that you enjoy, and keep your snowboarding muscles strong and flexible (see chapter 9 for ideas). Performing strength and conditioning exercises with a qualified trainer that you like and feel comfortable with can help you maintain your commitment and get the most out of your workouts. Working out with other athletes can make the experience more fun and keep you coming back for more.

Should the unthinkable happen and you sustain an injury, a reputable trainer can steer you toward medical evaluation if you need it and can help you rehab the injured area. Knowing when to ride through the pain and when not to push it will extend your longevity as a competitor. Once you step into the professional spotlight, you are hit with factors and pressures of all kinds, and you will need to know how to assess the situation and make the call to bow out if you aren't up to competing. As with any sport, when you compete with a serious injury, you put your career and your health on the line.

Just as using a trainer can make your time in the gym more productive, working with a coach can enhance your training time on the slopes. A well-qualified coach who has competition experience can guide you through new tricks and help you put together winning runs. The coach can quickly pinpoint exactly what you are doing wrong and explain how to make a change. Your coach should also be your mentor, someone you can trust to act in your best interests and help you succeed.

You may find a coach you like through your club or team. Most coaches have competed and know the ins and outs of what the judges are looking for. They are usually certified through a snowboard program and have a ton of experience in dialing in tricks and guiding you on a path to continue progressing and evolving as a rider. If your club or team has a coach who works with riders as a group, try a one-on-one session and see how you mesh together. You may be assigned to a coach via groups you are set in, but if it isn't a good fit, see if you can work with someone else. You may need to look outside of the club on your own to find someone who can help you on the side. Getting one-on-one coaching a few times a week from a knowledgeable and trusted coach is invaluable.

To continue your training, you can head to a facility specifically made for off-season snowboarding such as Woodward at Copper Mountain in Copper Mountain, Colorado, or Boreal Mountain Resort in Lake Tahoe, California. Woodward has an indoor year-round training facility built with dry slopes for practicing jibs and jumps. Both Woodward and Boreal offer camps and coaching year-round. Many pros head to Mount Hood in Oregon every summer. Both Windells and High Cascade have snowboard-specific camps near Mount Hood with private on-mountain parks. There are other options for snowboarding in the off-season in Canada and elsewhere, but if you really want to snowboard and train on snow in the northern hemisphere's summer months, you'll need to go down to New Zealand or South America. Both locations host a number of camps and training facilities for snowboarders of all abilities.

Once September hits it's time to start thinking about planning out your contest season in the north. Set a daily training and workout schedule. Set goals and find ways to accomplish them. Many riders work harder on their conditioning in the off months and then ease off before the start of the season. Exactly how much training and conditioning you do depends on whether you're female or male and how fit you already are, but setting some goals will help your overall riding performance.

As important as it is to work your body hard enough to stay fit and hone your skills, you must also give your body adequate time to rest, heal, and sleep. Lack of sleep not only zaps your energy but also impairs the ability of your muscles to recharge and recover. Feeling sluggish can interfere with your ability to focus and increases the risk of injuries. Getting eight hours of sleep, or however many hours you know your body needs to be fully rested, keeps you alert and at your best throughout the day, which is important in the days leading up to a contest, but also as a general practice. As recent studies show, you can't make up a long-term sleep deficit in a short period of time (www.scientificamerican.com/article.cfm?id=fact-or-fiction-can-you-catch-up-on-sleep).

Give your body short breaks during long practice sessions and between runs on the day of competition. Conserve some energy for the final event. How hard to go and how much energy to conserve depends on your personal level of fitness and how you are feeling. The best advice is to listen to what your body is telling you and pay attention to how it is reacting. If you know you are sore from previous days of riding and are already feeling sluggish, don't push it. Many factors can affect your body, but taking a day of rest in between long days of riding and competition or whenever you feel you need it will help keep you in good form.

Like rest and sleep, what you put into your body directly affects the way you perform. A nutritionist can give you advice on a diet that works for you. No matter what, don't skip breakfast. Get something in your system soon after you wake up, especially if you are competing that day. Eat something that has protein and will wake up your system. Heading to the hill on an empty stomach will only make you grumpy and irritable. Make sure you're on your A game by eating something nutritious. Bringing a few snacks to the hill is also a good idea. A piece of fruit, an energy bar, some nuts, or a half sandwich on whole-grain bread will give you a boost—and they won't spike your blood sugar and leave you feeling drained when it drops back down. Also, don't forget to stay hydrated. Drink plenty of water throughout the day.

Full-circle fitness is an even combination of both mental and physical readiness. Being confident and relaxed enables you to perform your best. Feeling and being fit is a major element, but your mind is also another strong factor in performance. Sometimes you may struggle to get past feeling tired and sore when you have to compete, and you have to rely on your mental strength. Don't show or tell anyone, including yourself, how bad you are feeling. The more you say it and think about it, the worse it will become. Unless you are seriously hurt, you can get past your physical challenges by working on your mental game. Talk yourself up. Remind yourself that you are capable and you have what it takes to get past anything. Being able to dig deep and do what you need to succeed when you are not at your best will help you become a stronger rider both mentally and physically.

Adopt the right mind-set as the season approaches. Write down what you hope to accomplish: places you want to travel, tricks you want to learn, contests you hope to enter, and so on. Look at and think about your goals daily to motivate yourself and to open your mind to the idea of achieving them. Be positive. Remember, you have to believe a thing is possible in order to actually do it. Reflect on what you've accomplished. Work on controlling your thoughts and emotions. Practice breathing exercises, and do some yoga if you enjoy it to put yourself in a calm state in which you can savor your experiences. You can tap into that calm, positive state later, when you are preparing to drop in at the biggest contest of the year!

Types of Freestyle Competitions

Competitions come in a variety of types to suit just about everyone's preferences. Some riders like to expand their skills and compete in different events, while others like to perfect what they know best. Most riders gravitate toward a particular type, but it can be fun to shake things up and do something new, too. Here are the most common types of freestyle snowboarding contests.

Rail Events

There are essentially two types of rail events: jams and contests. Rail jams have flourished in the past 10 years. This type of event is popular because it is entertaining to watch and the setup is easy for contest developers. At rail jams, competitors try to hit the feature or features as many times as they can in the allotted time frame. The rider is judged on overall performance instead of one trick, although there is usually a category for best trick as part of the prize purse. During a jam it doesn't necessarily matter how many times you are hitting the features in the time allotted; the degree of difficulty of the tricks you are landing and how clean you are in your style carry more weight. Although the effort of hitting the setup as many times as you can won't go unnoticed, if you aren't doing anything to back it up, it won't really do much for you besides make you tired.

For both rail jams and contests, the setup is usually a scaffolding that the riders can climb via stairs. There will be two or three features built on the metal scaffolding so riders can choose which feature they would like to hit. There is usually an easier feature and a few more challenging ones to mix it up. Variations such as an additional wall ride or feature at the bottom of the landing have also been seen in events. Snow is placed at the top of the features so riders can slide and turn into the setup, and there is a snow-filled landing.

Scaffolding setups have brought rail events to the general public because people don't need to be at the mountain to experience an event. Scaffolding setups can be brought into parking lots, stadiums, or just about anywhere. Rail events have been held in Las Vegas at the Hard Rock Hotel; in downtown Salt Lake City, Utah; at the beach in San Diego, California; and in downtown Seattle, Washington, to name a few. As long as snow can be farmed or made, a rail event is possible.

In jams, riders go one by one, either lined up or spread across the setup, dropping in one after another. Sometimes two riders will hit the setup at once if they are sessioning different features. The protocol is to call out when you are dropping so you don't cause a collision. Rail jams are visually fun to watch because there is so much action at once; contests have a more ordered approach as far as someone going when it is her turn and being eliminated during set heats.

Another type of rail event is an on-snow setup. The setups may include anything from a few rails and jibs in an enclosed area of the mountain to a well-developed production, with many rails, bonks, wall rides, and jibs. The variations are endless. It just really depends on how big the event is, who is sponsoring it, what the concept is, and whether the park builders at the resort can make it happen.

Rail jams and events start out on a small scale, with local riders and amateur contests, and go all the way to major operations, with pro riders who come in from around the world to be a part of the action. The status of the event and prize money involved are usually the biggest factors in determining the level of competition.

Most rail events and jams schedule some sort of practice or preliminary session before the finals. Depending on the event, riders may be scored by a panel of judges or by their peers.

It seems there is an endless number of rail events and jams of all types throughout the season. Some resorts may host one every week. It depends on budgeting and other factors, but rail contests are very popular on the snowboard scene. Big-name rail events include the X Games and U.S. Open, Ride Shakedown in Quebec and Washington, the West Coast Invitational in Mammoth, and the Volcom Peanut Butter Rail Jam series. The number of spectators depends on weather and location, but bigger events can bring several thousand spectators or more if they're live online or telecast.

Sometimes a winner is selected in a best overall format, and sometimes a winner is selected for best trick. What wins a rail contest really varies. But many factors come into play, whether it's an overall deal, best trick, or elimination-round contest. Creativity and skill, landing more difficult tricks switch, handplanting onto a feature and flipping off, and doing something that wows both the crowd and the judges are always taken into consideration.

To practice for rail events, ride the park rails and more difficult features to get super comfortable with hitting a variety of types. Most contest setups won't be ready until a few days before or even the day of the event, so being prepared by dialing in your skills on the most difficult rails you have access to is your best bet. If you can find out beforehand what features are going to be in the event, you can practice on similar ones. If you can't do that, try to ride with other competitors who can help you practice and lock in new rail tricks. Look at past winners and tricks, and learn as much as you can about what is expected and what might help you win. Think outside the box, and don't be afraid to put a twist on an average trick. Do things you know will set you apart, but know what you are capable of and stay within your boundaries.

Slopestyle Events

Slopestyle events consist of a variety of rails and jumps on a course. Slopestyle is by far the most versatile competition because the rider must be well rounded and creative in executing both jumps and rails. The general slopestyle setup is a few rails (usually two sets side by side so riders can hit whichever side they prefer), followed by another rail or jib section, ending with two or three jumps. There are variations, but overall the setup will begin with rails and end with jumps. There is usually a range of jibs to properly showcase different levels of skill and ability, and different features and jumps range from small to big. X Games–style events provide a range of jump sizes from 40 to 80-plus feet (12 to 24-plus m). The 2014 Winter Olympics in Russia will include an adapted version of this type of event. The specific setup at the Olympics is still to be determined, but it will be similar to the setup at main slope events.

Slopestyle events have surpassed many people's expectations, with male competitors landing triple corks and variations of the trick at practically every event. At pro events, male riders are expected to be able to land a series of double spins and variations on jumps and to have a strong technical style on rails. Riders must showcase a high level of difficulty and cleanliness of the run in order to make it in the top ranking. The level of riding is somewhat lower for women, but those who win are the ones doing a variety of switch tricks, cab spins on jumps, and 5s and 7s.

Slopestyle events always have a qualifying segment that takes place the day before the main event. Riders are allowed to practice on the course beforehand. Each rider usually gets two or three qualifying or semifinal runs that are judged based on technical tricks, variety, style, and amplitude. Competitors move on to the finals based on how well they did in the semis. Slopestyle events are geared for TV viewing because it's difficult to see the entire course from any position on the hill. The courses are almost always built specifically for the event, especially for contests such as the X Games and Dew Tour contests. The plans for the course are designed and developed months in advance. The setups are built on a closed run sometimes weeks before the event takes place. Regular riders visiting the resort aren't allowed to just session the setup. The course is built for the event only and is often torn down immediately afterward in order to prevent injuries.

It's difficult to practice for a course that has not yet been created or set up. Lapping parks and getting used to hitting several features in a row is good general preparation. Once you get to the competition course, you will be able to put together a run at practice and test the speed of the setup. Being able to hit a number of jib features in a series followed by jumps will help you prepare for competition. Most parks such as Northstar California in Tahoe; Mammoth Mountain in Mammoth Lakes, California; and Breckenridge in Breckenridge, Colorado, build a portion of their parks bigger than the rest and set it up similar to a slopestyle run.

Halfpipe

Halfpipe, or superpipe, as it is more commonly known, is one of the biggest events in snowboarding, if not the biggest. It's been an Olympic event since 1998. The pipe size ranges from 18 to 22 feet (5.5 to 6.7 m). Being able to have a decent pipe to practice in will make competing that much easier. Every pipe is a little different, so the more you are able to practice once you get there the better.

Most pipe events have a standard for tricks. For men, being able to land several double spins will up your score, while women are expected to complete a variety of technical spins including 7s and 9s, as well as underflips and switch spins. Both men and women must perform one straight air in their runs as well. Most pipe events are judged on a similar scale, and a variety of factors are considered. There is usually an elimination round with 20 to 30 riders, and the top 10 or so riders move on to the finals. Every contest is different in terms of how many athletes will move on. Each rider gets two or three runs in the prelims and in the finals, depending on the scope of the event. The best out of three is used to determine a winner. The highest score, usually out of 100, wins the event. A rider may or may not perform the same run each time depending on how he is feeling; he might add more technical tricks if he landed his first run well or take an easier route if he didn't.

Riders are judged on overall performance, but the riders who score the highest are the ones launching the biggest out of the pipe (amplitude); trying the most technical and difficult tricks; showing the best style (including grabs and body position during tricks); and of course, landing solidly on every hit, without hitting the deck of the pipe, washing out, or landing flat-bottom. If a rider lands but drags a hand slightly on the

Hannah Teter in the pipe at the Winter Dew Tour competition.

snow, points can be deducted. Variety and difficulty of tricks are just the beginning. Being able to get air high out of the pipe and being able to put a complete run together with style is what encourages the judges to award higher scores.

Just like competing in any other type of contest, watching events, learning what is expected, and being able to perform under competitive conditions are what will make you a great halfpipe rider. Practicing with a coach who knows the judging criteria and continuing to attempt various tricks will help you succeed. As always, practice makes perfect, so get out there and keep after it. Put a solid run together and perfect it. Your hard work will pay off.

Big Air Events

Big air events have become a huge spectator sport. These events consist of one massive jump, where the rider performs one trick. These are usually male-only contests because of the severity of the feature, although women sometimes participate. It depends on the event, the setup, and whether a prize is offered for the top female competitor. As of late, the winning trick in big air competitions is a triple cork. Accomplished a few seasons ago by Norwegian Torstein Horgmo during the X Games, this trick has since been done by a number of riders, and variations such as switch, front, and back are also performed.

Most riders in this event also compete in slopestyle, and a handful compete in pipe, which makes sense because big air is a sector of slopestyle, although it is of higher consequence. The difference is in the sheer size of the jump, which includes a massive drop-in from the top of a 10-story-plus scaffolding at some events and a steep, hard landing onto a hand-built surface with snow covering it. Big air competitions at the X Games and other events on snow feature a similar jump of up to 100 feet (30 m), built on a more forgiving snow landing. Riders don't usually drop from a scaffolding, either; they just ride in from the top of a run. A lot of big air events are held in an arena-size facility where thousands of spectators come to watch, and the scaffoldings are built specifically for the competition. Snow is farmed in or blown by machines before the event.

Riders in big air contests are judged on amplitude, the trick itself, style, landing well, and riding away clean. Riders get two or three runs to land their best trick. The best run counts. Practicing for big air is probably more difficult than for any other discipline. Access to huge jumps is a factor. Most resorts don't want to build jumps of such consequence because they don't want to take on the liability issues. Riders usually practice on the biggest slopestyle jump available. Once the course is open to contestants, they can practice and get to know the setup and speed before the actual competition.

Big Mountain

Another growing trend in competitions is big mountain events. These events are more of a grassroots style of competition held on steeper, more advanced runs at specific resorts. Examples of this type of event include the Freeride World Tour, which is held at Squaw Valley in Tahoe and a number of other locations throughout the season and the North Face Masters, a three-stop tour held at Snowbird, Utah; Kirkwood, California; and Crystal Mountain, Washington. The number of contests throughout the season currently seems to be somewhat less than any other discipline, but support from backcountry sponsors and more advanced mountain venues continues to build. As backcountry snowboarding has grown, big mountain freestyle events that challenge riders to choose a line down the mountain and ride it well have been developed. The focus is not on performing the gnarliest trick, it's on how you ride what's in front of you and how you handle the terrain. The contest is held in a confined and controlled environment; the idea is to showcase the best big mountain riders. Judging is based on the riders' choice of line, how they ride the line down (fast, big and small turns, how much control they have), what tricks they perform, and how clean the run is.

During most big mountain events, riders are given a practice day to get to know the terrain and choose their lines, an elimination day to narrow the field of riders, and a day of finals. During the finals, riders are given two or three runs to perform their best and impress the judges. Spectators are welcome, although getting to some of the locations is sometimes challenging. The event is often filmed from the top and bottom of the course for the Web. The majority of big mountain events are not televised for advertising reasons. Big mountain contests are for riders who like to perform in a less hectic, less commercialized environment. The stakes are higher in some ways because avalanches are a potential consequence, even though the site is managed by the ski patrol, and because it is difficult to judge the line properly and assess it from below.

Riders enter most big mountain events by applying on a specific date. You don't have to do anything special to qualify, you just need to enter before the limited number of slots (usually 20 to 50) fills up. Men and women compete in separate categories.

Finding Yourself as a Snowboarder

Snowboarding is an endless endeavor. That's what makes it so fun. There are so many different aspects and disciplines. You will find that some are more fun and come more naturally to you, while others are more challenging and not as thrilling. We've touched on many aspects of the sport, but there are so many other facets of snowboarding, and they continue to expand as the sport evolves. As you continue on your snowboarding journey, you will no doubt find more tricks to master, other ways to compete, and an unlimited number of little pieces of information to help you along your way.

We hope you will take the information we've provided and make it your own. Take what you've learned here, combine it with the exciting personal discoveries that await you, and reach for your own version of snowboarding greatness.

Whether your goal is sliding down the mountain, hitting your first rail, dropping into and airing out of your first 22-foot halfpipe, or finally knowing what it's like to pick a perfect powder line and ride it with ease, go for it. You don't have to do anything other than what makes you happy. Snowboarding is what you want to make it. It's a one-of-a-kind experience that's different and personal for everyone who encounters it, yet it brings so many of us closer together through our bond and love for the snow, nature, and the mountains. This guide is meant to help you reach your ultimate potential. Mastering snowboarding may mean something different to everyone, but developing your potential is the best part. From first-timers to professionals, the goal is to explore, challenge, and push yourself, for yourself. Always remember that. When you find yourself laughing, smiling, and enjoying yourself out on the slopes, wave hi to us. You can now call yourself a snowboarder.

GLOSSARY

air—Any time you are not touching the ground with your snowboard, you are getting air.

backcountry—Any terrain outside of a resort's boundary line. Backcountry terrain is accessible on foot or by snowmobile, splitboard, helicopter, and so on. There is no avalanche control in the backcountry, and you are entering at your own risk.

backside—Spinning or performing a trick, turning backward or uphill, is considered backside.

bindings—The metal or plastic pieces that screw into the holes on your snowboard so you can strap your feet in. There are two bindings, a right and a left, and each is accompanied by a one- or two-strap ratchet system in order for you to lock your foot in place.

board—The short term for a snowboard.

boardslide—A rail trick that positions the front of your body downhill while your board is positioned as a T on the feature.

boots—The snowboard-specific footwear you use to have better traction on snow and more stability when you're strapped onto your snowboard.

boxes—Features or obstacles that are found in the terrain park of a resort. They are a long, narrow rectangle made of wood that stands off the ground. The top of the box is built with plexiglass or some form of material that makes sliding on it with a board easy. Boxes can come in a variety of designs, shapes, and sizes.

Burton Snowboards—The biggest brand in snowboarding, founded by Jake Burton Carpenter in 1977 out of a barn in Vermont. The brand is known worldwide by its B symbol and is one of the biggest innovators on the technical side of the sport.

cab—Switch frontside spins off of a feature.

camber—A design shape in a snowboard that bows from tip to tail in an upward arch. Camber is used to create more response while riding.

deck—Another term for a snowboard. "Grab your deck and let's hit the slopes."

demo—A setup of snowboards, boots, bindings, and accessories on display in the parking lot or in an area of a resort where people can borrow and try them out. The product may or may not be for sale on-site, but demos give people interested in new products a chance to try different stuff.

detune—The term used for taking a file or a grinder to the metal of your edges to take away the sharpness of the edge, which gives it a less responsive and forgiving feel.

drop-in—The starting point before you ride into a jump or feature of any kind. A rider will call, "Dropping!" to let others know he is taking his turn and about to ride toward the feature.

EST—A binding system designed by Burton Snowboards that is composed of sliders in the two binding points that slide from tip to tail, which enables an almost infinite number of stance options.

feature—Jumps, rails, boxes, jibs, wall rides, and anything built by a machine and put in the park. Some people also refer to natural hits, tree jibs, wind lips, cliffs, and so on as features.

flat-bottom—The bottom of a pipe or jump that you use to ride into another feature or ride away from a landing.

flex—How boots, bindings, and boards perform in terms of feeling soft and loose or stiff and aggressive. Boards, boots, and bindings are often rated on a scale of 1 to 10, softest to stiffest, so a rider will know the type of flex.

forward lean—A technical feature on bindings used to push the highback forward, which in turn naturally bends the rider's knees into a lower position. There is usually a ratchet or other way to adjust the forward lean on the back of the binding.

freeride—A type of riding style that refers to riding the entire mountain and all types of terrain. Freeriders often carve big mountains and ride terrain out of bounds. Freeride is also used to describe product that is made for freeride terrain.

freestyle—A type of snowboarding that refers to getting loose, doing tricks, and being innovative with new tricks. Freestyle is a style of snowboarding that encourages being free, doing what you feel, and putting your own twist on your skills. Snowboard equipment is often labeled freestyle to help the buyer understand that the product can be used in a variety of conditions and not just one specific area.

frontside—Spinning or performing a trick, turning forward or downhill, is considered frontside.

goggles—Eye protection designed to fit around the face, specifically made to use while snowboarding to protect from glare, sun, and snow.

goofy-footed—Anyone who rides with their right foot in front as their lead foot is considered goofy-footed.

halfpipe—Built out of snow, a halfpipe is built in the ground as a feature at resorts. The halfpipe has two walls and a flat-bottom adjoining them. Riders ride up the wall and perform tricks out of the pipe. They ride it similar to a wave, carving back and forth on both walls.

hard goods—Snowboards, boots, and bindings.

hardpack—A term used to describe the snow when it is firm. Hardpack snow usually occurs after it freezes overnight, but it will usually thaw out during the day if the weather is warm.

heli—The short term for a helicopter.

highback—The back piece of the binding that holds your heel and ankle upright.

insert—A footbed or some sort of supportive foam piece used to help support the arch and shape of your foot. Inserts can help with balance, prevent injuries, and make the boots fit the foot better.

Jake Burton Carpenter—The man who founded Burton Snowboards and helped develop the snowboard we currently ride today. He was one of the first producers of snowboards and continues to be a leader in the snowboard world on all fronts.

landing—Although not always marked, the area where a rider should land on the snowboard after hitting a jump, jib, or any feature.

liner—A shell insert that is removable inside the outer shell of a snowboard boot. It is used for more support, comfort, and ventilation.

lip—The edge of a jump or pipe where you take off is called the lip.

locking on—Securing yourself on a rail and feeling in control. You are locked on once you get onto the feature and are sliding it.

noboarding—Riding a board without bindings. Your feet are not attached, so it is more like skating on the snow, but usually there will be a rope attached that you can use to turn and go fast.

nose slide—A trick performed on a jib or flat ground where a rider presses all his weight forward on the nose (or front) of the board and slides on a feature or ground with the tail (or back) of the board lifted off the ground.

off-piste—Another term for out-of-bounds riding. If something is off-piste, it is off the beaten path and isn't bombed frequently to prevent avalanches. It is at-your-own-risk terrain.

ollie—The basis of all tricks is the ollie. The movement of jumping off the group in the air is an ollie.

outerwear—Any jacket or pants you wear on the slopes. Snowboard-specific outerwear is usually insulated, water proofed, seamed, and sealed to help a rider stay dry, warm, and comfortable.

park—An area or run where there are hand-built features including jumps, rails, jibs, and boxes, usually found at resorts in bounds. There may be several parks on a mountain, and all are usually distinctly marked by class, from beginner to advanced.

powder—The term used to describe fresh snow. Anytime there is a significant amount of new snow overnight or during the day, it's called powder. Many riders live for powder days, where they can ride fresh ungroomed runs.

prespinning—The setup of a trick before you come off a jump when you twist your arms and body in preparation is considered prespinning.

protection—Any type of gear that helps protect you in wintery conditions and prevent you from getting injured. Examples include helmets, impact shorts (which are worn under pants to add padding), mouth guards, spine protectors, and wrist guards.

quarterpipe—A snow feature built with a drop-in and a lip that a rider can launch off of. A quarterpipe resembles a halfpipe, except there is only one side to it.

rail—Any round or flat piece of metal that has been built by welders and made specifically for a snowboarder to perform tricks on.

Recco—A tracking device inserted into the fabric of certain garments that sends a signal traceable by beacons in order to find a missing person. It is found in many products on the market as an extra precaution in case a person is missing or buried in the snow.

regular-footed—Any rider who rides with their left foot in front as their lead foot is considered regular-footed.

reverse camber—A design shape (opposite of camber) that has a reverse bow from tip to tail, creating a loose and less responsive feel while riding. Reverse-camber boards are most common nowadays, since they are easier to ride for most.

run-in—The path to the feature or obstacle that a person is hitting. For example, if you were hitting a jump, the path into the jump is referred to as the run-in where you get the speed to hit the jump.

setup—Usually refers to your board and binding combination. "What setup do you have?"

Sherman Poppen—The man who is said to have founded the sport of snowboarding back in 1965.

slopes—The runs on the mountain are considered slopes. "Hitting the slopes" is a common phrase.

Snurfer—The original term for the snowboard, named by Poppen. It means a board used to surf on the snow. The Snurfer was one piece of flat wood with a rope attached and was used to slide and turn on the snow.

soft goods—Jackets, pants, gloves, goggles, and any other snowboard accessory that is soft.

speed-check—A rider may slow down or speed up while approaching a jump to get the feel of the speed needed to perform a trick.

Speed Zone—A lacing system used in many boots that makes it faster and easier to lace and unlace boots and tighten or loosen certain areas of a rider's boots for a custom fit.

superpipe—Any halfpipe that has walls of 18 feet (5.5 m) or higher. A superpipe is used for all major competitions and continues to get bigger in size.

swampfoot—This is when you're bummed out because your feet feel as if they have been in a hot tub for a week. Swampfoot is caused by shredding or walking around too much in the snow or in wet conditions. There is no real way to prevent it if you are wearing your boots for an extended period of time.

switch—Anytime a snowboarder rides with the opposite foot forward from the normal lead foot.

tabletops—Jumps are considered tabletops.

tail slide—sliding a rail, box, or similar feature with the back or tail of the board is called a tail slide.

takeoff—The run-in turns into the takeoff of a feature or obstacle. It's the last part of the snow you ride before you are either in the air off of a jump or on a rail or box.

transition—The transition, or tranny, is the slope of the jump a snowboarder rides onto before hitting the lip of the jump.

waxing—Riders wax the base, or bottom, of their boards so they go faster and are more consistent. Bases tend to dry out as they are used, so riders use a cube of wax and a heated iron to melt wax onto them. After the wax has dried, riders should scrape it off with a plastic or metal scraper to even and smooth it out.

white room—Riding through a cloud or tunnel of snow that is created by a turn you have made. Usually you are in the white room on a powder day since there is fresh snow, and when you make a hard turn it will create a wave of snow over you.

ABOUT THE AUTHORS

Hannah Teter is one of the greatest female snowboarders in the history of the sport, having earned numerous awards and honors since she began competitive snowboarding at the age of 15, when she placed fourth in her first world cup halfpipe event. She has represented the United States twice in the Winter Olympic Games, medaling both times in the halfpipe. She earned the gold medal in 2006, for which the United States Olympic Committee named her the USOC Sportswoman of the Year, and the silver medal in 2010. She has achieved six FIS Snowboard world cup victories and earned bronze at the 2005 FIS world championships. Competing in the Winter X Games, Hannah has medaled five times, winning the gold for the superpipe in 2003 and bronze in 2004, 2005, 2009, and 2010.

Hannah's snowboarding record is legendary, and her mainstream celebrity acknowledgments include a 2006 ESPN ESPY Award for Best Female Action Sport Athlete, a 2010 appearance in *Sports Illustrated*'s famed swimsuit issue, and a Ben & Jerry's Ice Cream flavor named in her honor, Hannah Teter's Maple Blondie. She is active in philanthropy and is committed to helping the world's poor. She founded Hannah's Gold (www.hannahsgold.com) in 2008, and the charity donates profits from her family's Vermont maple syrup sales to the village of Kirindon, Kenya, to help provide clean drinking water, farming opportunities, and schooling for the village. In 2010 she launched Sweet Cheeks, a charity that donates 40 percent of proceeds to Children International. Hannah often donates her prize money from competitions to her charity. Hannah was awarded a VH1 Do Something Award in the category of Do Something Athlete.

Hannah lives in Belmont, Vermont.

Tawnya Schultz is the founder and editor of *Tahoe Snowboard* magazine, which recently celebrated its third season of publication. She is a contributor to *Snowboard* magazine (for which she has managed three women's annuals) and is a weekly writer for burtongirls.com. Tawnya has written for *Cooler Mag, Transworld Snowboarding,* and *Snowboarder* magazine while also running her own website, www.tawnya.us. She is the author of a children's snowboarding book titled *Sammy the Shredder*, which tells the story of Sammy a snowboarding bear.

Tawnya lives in Kings Beach, California.

You'll find other outstanding outdoor sports resources at

www.HumanKinetics.com/outdoorsports

In the U.S. call 1-800-747-4457

Australia 08 8372 0999 • Canada 1-800-465-7301
Europe +44 (0) 113 255 5665 • New Zealand 0800 222 062

HUMAN KINETICS
The Premier Publisher for Sports & Fitness
P.O. Box 5076 • Champaign, IL 61825-5076 USA

eBook
available at
HumanKinetics.com